Life on a low income

D1313415

Elaine Kempson

The **Joseph Rowntree Foundation** has supported this project as part of its programme of research and innovative development projects, which it hopes will be of value to policy makers and practitioners. The facts presented and views expressed in this report are, however, those of the author and not necessarily those of the Foundation.

N 305 569
405495

Published by YPS for the Joseph Rowntree Foundation

ISBN 1 899987 17 7

Prepared and printed by:
York Publishing Services Ltd
64 Hallfield Road
Layerthorpe
York YO3 7XQ

Cover photos: Melanie Friend and Joanne O'Brien, Format Partners

Contents

Acknowledgements   viii

Foreword   ix

Summary   xi

Introduction   1

PART ONE

1   Making ends meet   15
     Developing money management skills   15
     Patterns of money management   17
     Approaches to money management   17
     Current accounts and cash budgets   19
     Setting priorities   19
     Cutting out 'luxuries'   20
     Other non-essentials   21
     Saving money on essentials   23
     Food   23
     Clothes   25
     Making difficult choices   25
     Dynamics of making ends meet   27
     Summary   28

2   Life on a low income   30
     Impact on family life   30
     Poor diet   32
     School meals   33
     Achieving a healthy diet   34
     Restricted use of fuel and water   34
     Heating   34
     Water   35
     Debt   36
     Stigma of poverty and debt   36
     Debt recovery practices   37
     Disconnection and repossesion   39

Poor health   40
    Links with diet   40
    Importance of heating   42
    Effects of poor housing and homelessness   42
    Money worries   43
Summary   45

3 **Varying experiences of poverty**   46
Income levels   46
Length of time on a low income   47
Approaches to making ends meet   49
Family circumstances   50
    Costs of setting up home   50
    The costs of children   52
    Having someone to share the problems with   55
Health and disability   57
Family and support networks   57
    Help with 'luxuries'   58
    Help with furniture and household equipment   58
    Help with making ends meet   59
    Limitations on help   60
Locality and neighbourhood   61
    Variations in the cost of living   61
    Inner city housing estates and rural villages   62
Time of the year   64
Experience of poverty within the household   65
    Men   65
    Women   66
    Children   67
Summary   68

PART TWO

4 **Changes in the labour market**   73
High unemployment   74
    The commitment to work   75
    Barriers to working   77
        Unskilled workers   77
        Age   77
        Poor health and disability   78
        Women returners   78
    Retraining   79

Changing nature of jobs   81
    Part-time employment   81
    Temporary jobs   82
    Working in the informal economy   83
    Low pay   85
Tackling low wages   86
    In-work benefits   86
    Minimum wage   86
       Calculations by people out of work   87
       Earnings that need to be supplemented   87
       Incomes needed to avoid financial difficulties 87
       Minimum wage level   88
Increasing polarisation between two-earner and no-earner households   89
Summary   91

5 Housing policy   93
Shifts in tenure   94
    Access to social rented housing   95
       Long waiting lists   95
       Do teenage mothers queue jump?   96
       Specific areas of shortfall   97
    Increasing polarisation between neighbourhoods   98
    Deregulation of the private rented sector   99
       Access for people living on low incomes 100
       Rents and Housing Benefit restrictions 100
       Insecurity and disrepair   102
    Problematic home ownership   102
       Rural areas   102
       Low-income home buyers   103
       Mortgage arrears and possessions   103
       Negative equity   104
Increases in homelessness   105
    The causes of homelessness   105
    Statutory homelessness   105
    Single homelessness   106
    People with special needs   110
Changes in housing subsidies   111
    Tenants   111
       Unemployment trap   112
       Housing Benefit poverty trap   112
    Homebuyers   113

Summary 113

6 Consumer credit and household utilities 115
Consumer credit 115
    Use of credit 115
        Consumer goods 116
        Household goods and necessities 116
        Smoothing income fluctuations 117
        Paying bills 118
    Dual credit market 119
    Financial exclusion 121
    Over-commitment 123
Household utilities 123
    Charges 123
    Payment facilities 125
    Debt recovery 126
    Universal access 127
    Role of the regulators 127
Summary 128

7 Social security and fiscal policy 129
Fiscal changes 129
    Shift towards indirect taxation 129
    Local taxes 130
Benefit levels 131
Social security reform 132
    Income Support 133
    Social Fund 135
    Work expenses and childcare costs 137
    Family Credit 138
    Sickness and disability benefits 139
    Child Support Agency 141
Benefit administration 143
    Introduction of changes 143
    Errors and delays 143
    Changes in circumstances 144
    Frequency of benefit payments 144
    Direct payments from benefit 145
    Information and advice 145
    Benefit take-up 146
        Lack of knowledge 147

Reluctance to claim   149
Language problems   150
Current concerns   151
Rising costs   151
Proofs of job search   152
Moves towards private insurance and pensions   153
Fraud   155
Social security and social change   156
Labour markets   157
Housing   157
Care in the community   158
Privatisation of utilities   158
Summary   159

PART THREE

8 Conclusions and policy implications   163
Finding and keeping a job   163
Lack of jobs   164
Low pay   164
Temporary and part-time jobs   166
Tackling non-financial barriers to work   166
A decent home   167
Need for rented housing   167
Changes in housing subsidies   167
Limits to home ownership   168
An adequate income   168
Reversing the growth in income inequalities   169
Revising the benefits system   169
Social security and wider social and economic change   170
Making ends meet   172
Giving more control to claimants   172
Combating exclusion   173
Social exclusion   173
Homelessness and marginalised areas   174
Financial exclusion   174
Exclusion from the consumer society   174
Offering hope for the future   175

References   177
Appendix   181

Acknowledgements

A book of this kind is the result of contributions from many people. I owe a considerable debt to the researchers who undertook the studies on which this book is based. The high quality of their work meant that I had a wealth of information on which to draw. I hope I have been able to do justice to their efforts.

The different studies would not have been possible without the willing co-operation of over 2,100 people. The fact that they were prepared to talk in detail about their circumstances has provided a clear insight into the realities of life on a low income. I hope I have been able to convey an accurate picture on their behalf.

Throughout the project I was able to draw upon the advice of a number of experts associated with the study: Barbara Ballard, Fran Bennett, John Hills, Peter Kemp, Jan Pahl, David Utting, Robert Walker and Derek Williams. They read draft chapters in detail and without their comments and criticisms this book would have been a great deal poorer.

Foreword

A year ago the Joseph Rowntree Foundation's *Inquiry into Income and Wealth* reported on the social and economic changes that have divided Britain between a comfortable majority and a large and growing minority who are denied a stake in increasing national prosperity. It issued a stark warning that society will pay a heavy price in terms of extra public spending, wasted human resources and the collapse of communities if it fails to bring this excluded minority back into the mainstream.

The *Inquiry* found that despite previous claims that higher incomes for the rich would in due course benefit the poor, no evidence could be found for a 'trickle down' effect. Indeed, on two different measures of net income, the poorest 10 per cent of households had either stood still in real terms or declined. Still more disturbing was the evidence that low income households include a rising and disproportionate number of children.

Yet statistics barely lift the curtain on the day to day reality of life for the millions of individuals and families at the bottom of the economic pile. That is the immense value of this new report by Elaine Kempson which skilfully draws together the threads from more than 30 qualitative studies in which people speak for themselves. Irrespective of how they define 'poverty', no-one reading this report can be left in doubt that life on a low income in 1990s Britain is a stressful and debilitating experience. People who rely on Income Support, in particular, face a struggle against encroaching debt and social isolation where even the most resilient and resourceful are hard pressed to survive.

One important message to emerge is that those caught in the exclusion zone cannot be stigmatised and dismissed as an 'underclass' whose aspirations are somehow different from those of the majority. Beyond that, however, the report identifies the stumbling blocks and traps within policy that currently deny those aspirations, in terms of income, employment and housing. It demonstrates, for example, how a sum as modest as £15 a week extra can make the difference between sink or swim for those on very low incomes. Better still, it sets out policy options for achieving it.

Many of the people whose voices are heard in this report say they can see little hope of improvement in own their lives or, more alarmingly, those of their children. The future welfare of the whole of our society depends on whether we can now find the determination to ensure that their deep pessimism proves unfounded.

Sir Peter Barclay,
Chairman, Joseph Rowntree Foundation

 # Summary

Making ends meet

People living on low incomes show great resilience and resourcefulness as they try to make ends meet. Most people learn how to manage their budgets through a process of trial and error. So the longer they have lived on a low income, the better they get at making ends meet.

Managing on a low income requires great skill: costing and controlling a tight budget; setting priorities; juggling bills; making difficult choices; cutting out all but the essentials and sometimes going without these necessities too. Women, who generally manage the budget, bear the brunt of these continual worries.

Life on a low income

Making ends meet on a low income means going without. It generally means having no social life, with families spending a lot of time at home together. This can cement relationships but more often it places a strain on them, resulting in family breakdown in extreme cases.

It leads to poor diets, with choices between eating healthy foods or having sufficient to eat, and to economies in the use of heating and water. These, in turn, contribute to health problems, as does inadequate housing. People living on state benefits usually have insufficient income to cover even their basic needs. As a consequence they face a difficult choice between paying their bills on time and having adequate food and heating. Yet, as little as £15 extra a week can mean that they can avoid such difficult choices.

Money worries are common in low-income households, but debts mainly occur through lack of money rather than poor budgeting or attempts to avoid payment. Unsympathetic creditors can add to the anxieties people face, so that debt, too, takes a toll on people's health.

Varying experiences of poverty

While the consequences of living on a low income are wide-ranging, individual experiences of poverty differ depending on people's circumstances. Factors that can compound an already difficult situation include: the length of time people have been poor; the approach they take to making ends meet; their family circumstances; ill-health and disability; having no-one to turn to for financial help; the neighbourhood they live in; and even the time of the year.

Impact of social and economic change

People who live on low incomes are not an underclass. They have aspirations just like others in society: they want a job, a decent home, and an income that is enough to pay the bills with a little to spare. But social and economic changes that have benefited the majority of the population, increasing their incomes and their standard of living, have made life more difficult for a growing minority, whose fairly modest aspirations are often beyond their reach.

Those who are out of work or have low-paid jobs have seen their incomes grow least because of fiscal and social security changes. They have the most limited access to housing and financial services, and are hit hardest by rises in basic household bills.

Changes in the labour market

Most people view a job as the only way they can secure an adequate income. They do not want hand-outs or to be dependent on the state, but to be able to provide for themselves and their families. They consequently go to great lengths to find a job, especially if they are the main breadwinner. But they face a number of barriers to earning a living. Unskilled manual workers have a high risk of getting into a downward spiral of increasing job insecurity and falling wage levels. Young people leaving school, older workers, ethnic minorities, people in poor health or with disabilities, and women trying to return to the labour market all seem to fare badly in the current labour market – especially if they have limited skills.

As a result, there is a growing group of people who have not had 'a proper job' for years and can see no prospect of getting one in the future. Statistics show that most unemployed people do not remain out of work for long periods. But the qualitative research reveals an alternation between unemployment and low-paid work, with no real escape from life on a low income.

And, since low-skilled workers tend to marry other workers with low skills, these trends are magnified at the household level where there is growing polarisation between those with two wage earners and those with none.

People are expected to be flexible in their approach to the job market, taking temporary and short-term jobs, and those offering a few hours work per week. But the social security system, as it stands, is not flexible enough to accommodate these jobs. People who take them benefit very little financially, unless they commit fraud.

Unemployed people's wage aspirations are generally modest (they typically want just enough to cover their basic outgoings) and there is little evidence that they are pricing themselves out of the job market. But wage levels are often too low to meet these needs and there is a reluctance to take such low-paid jobs or ones that do not offer some degree of financial security. Even so, people *do* take them if they think they might lead onto a better paid or more secure job, or if they have opportunities for increasing their income – by working overtime, taking a second job or, in couples, their partner working as well.

Housing policy

People want a home that is affordable, large enough for their needs, in a reasonable state of repair, and in an area where fears of crime and vandalism do not dominate their lives. Yet changes in housing policy have meant that a growing number of people are unable to achieve these aspirations.

While most people are adequately housed, there has been a long-term upward trend in street homelessness – often affecting vulnerable people, so that poor health and homelessness become inextricably linked. Homeless people face a poverty cycle of 'no home, no job, no home', which requires concerted efforts to be broken.

There is also a growing concentration of high unemployment, low incomes and lone parenthood in particular neighbourhoods and on particular housing estates. High levels of crime and vandalism add greatly to the problems people already face. They become afraid to go out, live in fear and face a high risk of theft.

Rising rents and shifts from bricks and mortar subsidies to personal means-tested benefits have made it more difficult for tenants to escape from poverty. At the same time, the extension of home ownership to people with low incomes or in insecure jobs has resulted in rising mortgage arrears and possessions. For a minority of people whose homes have been repossessed leaving them with negative equity, home ownership has acted as a route into poverty and long-term indebtedness.

Consumer credit and household utilities

Most people have benefited greatly from the deregulation of financial institutions. More sophisticated screening of applicants, however, means that many people on low incomes either have no access to high street financial services or find they do not cater for their needs. Where alternatives are available, they usually involve additional costs. People without bank accounts face charges for cashing cheques or making payments through post offices, and cannot take advantage of reduced tariffs for paying bills on direct debit. Loans from local moneylenders cost considerably more than credit from high street financial institutions. People living in high crime neighbourhoods are often denied access even to licensed moneylenders and frequently have no option but to turn to unlicensed loan sharks and pay huge financial and other costs.

Likewise, privatisation of the utilities has not always benefited low-income consumers. The price of gas and electricity may have dropped slightly (discounting the effect of VAT), but water charges have risen appreciably. Moreover, the more commercial approach being taken by some utility companies to bill-payment facilities and debt recovery has hit low-income consumers the hardest. There are also concerns about poor people retaining access to essential services, as the utilities are opened up to competition.

Social security and fiscal policy

Shifts from direct to indirect taxation have widened income inequalities, while reforms of local taxation (and the introduction of the Poll Tax in particular) have placed a further strain on the budgets of people living on low incomes.

The decision to uprate benefits in line with prices has led to incomes of the poorest households falling further behind the rest of the population. Restraint on public expenditure has put the social security budget under constant scrutiny, with many changes taking place to try to contain spending and target it on those in greatest need. This has led to winners and losers.

For example, the introduction of Family Credit has helped low-waged families with children. But the removal of entitlement to Income Support for 16 and 17 year olds, and the introduction of the Social Fund to replace single payments, have clearly caused problems for others.

Important changes to the administration of benefit payments have, on balance, improved the service to claimants. These include the setting up of a range of agencies to administer social security payments at 'arm's length' from the Department of Social Security.

Other administrative changes have made budgeting more difficult for claimants, including the decision to pay most benefits fortnightly and in arrears and the increased use of direct payments from benefit. The provision of information and advice by the Benefits Agency and non-take-up of benefit are two areas where progress has been made, but much still remains to be done.

Lack of a co-ordinated approach to policy

The lack of a co-ordinated approach to policy-making has often added to the problems faced by people on low incomes.

Economic policies of Government and employers have increased the numbers of people who claim social security, either because they cannot find work at all or they can only get a low-paid job. This, in turn, has led to restrictions on the eligibility of unemployed and sick or disabled people for insurance-based benefits and a tightening of the criteria for benefit entitlement generally.

Shifts in housing subsidies have led to a large increase in rents and Housing Benefit expenditure, which has, in turn, led to a series of measures designed to cut the budget.

Encouragement of low-income home ownership at a time of growing job insecurity has increased Income Support expenditure on assistance with mortgage interest payments. This has led to restrictions in the availability of state assistance and an encouragement of private insurance provision. Many people on low incomes or in insecure jobs find that private insurance is not available when they most need it.

The policy of care in the community has shifted costs from the health service to the social security and local authority budgets. At the same time, controls on local authority spending mean that many people (including those on benefit) now have to contribute to the costs of assistance that they would previously have received free.

Privatisation of the former public utilities has brought a more commercial approach to their services. It is widely believed, in the privatised utilities, that cross-subsidies should be phased out and the social security system should ensure that poor people are able to pay their bills. The experience with rising water bills must cast doubt on whether this will be the case.

Many of these changes have been designed to cut overall public spending and to deliver a higher standard of living to the majority of the population. In the process they have increased social security expenditure and led to demands for this spending to be contained. It is those living on the lowest incomes who ultimately pay the price.

The policy response

A co-ordinated response – from government, local authorities and commercial companies – is required to ensure that people on low incomes can benefit from general rises in living standards and do not become an excluded minority. The aspirations of poor people identify five main areas where more could be done to improve their lives:

Jobs: increasing the number of jobs; tackling low pay; increasing the flexibility of the benefits system to accommodate the jobs being created; and tackling the non-financial barriers to work.

Homes: expanding the rental sector at rents that are affordable; more flexible approaches to tenure; and ensuring adequate safeguards for home buyers on low incomes or in insecure jobs.

Incomes: reversing the growth in income inequalities; simplifying the benefits system, making it easier for people to move into work and ensuring adequate benefit levels for long-term claimants; more consideration of the consequences of social and economic changes for the benefits system to avoid even greater hardship for claimants.

Making ends meet: addressing the trends in benefit administration which have reduced the control that claimants have over their budgets.

Exclusion: combating social exclusion; tackling homelessness and marginalised areas; ensuring universal access to financial services and household utilities; and allowing poor people to benefit from the consumer society.

Above all there is a need to re-establish hope in the lives of people on low-incomes – both for themselves and for their children.

Introduction

About 14 million people – one in four of the British population – live in households with incomes that are below half the national average. Among them are 9.8 million people who live on the benefit safety net provided by Income Support (DSS, 1994). Since 1979, the number of people living on such low incomes has trebled and income inequalities have increased. But what does this mean for the millions of individuals who make up the statistics?

A year ago, the Joseph Rowntree Foundation's *Inquiry into Income and Wealth* expressed grave concern about these trends and identified the dangers of social dislocation if such a large section of the population continued to be denied a stake in national prosperity. This report builds on that work to explore exactly what life is like for people who live on low incomes. It does so by drawing together the findings of a number of recent research studies which have explored, in depth, various aspects of the lives of low-income households. In doing this, the intention is to provide a detailed picture of what it means to live in Britain's poorest households in the mid–1990s.

Who are the low-income households?

As the case studies included in this section suggest, people living on low incomes are a diverse group, spanning all ages and all family circumstances. They include people in work and those not working, and can be found living in a wide range of neighbourhoods.

The majority (over half) of low-income households are families with dependent children, with the number of low-income families (and of lone parent families in particular) growing rapidly in the 1980s. At the same time the proportion of pensioners among those on low incomes fell to about two out of ten, reflecting the wider access to occupational pension schemes. Even so, pensioners are still over-represented in the lowest income groups (Figure 1).

The number of households with low earnings from work has also grown and they account for three out of ten of those living on incomes below half the national average. But the biggest changes have been among those who are not working. Since the end of the 1970s, there has been a substantial increase in the proportions of people of working age who are unemployed or who are not working in the labour force – because they are long-term sick or disabled or because they are lone parents. People who are unemployed or economically inactive each account for more than two out of ten of those living on low incomes (Figure 2). The risks of unemployment or low-waged work are highest for people with limited skills, and for long-term sick and disabled people and people from ethnic minority communities who all face considerable discrimination in the labour market.

Figure 1 Family and personal circumstances

(a) Households below half average
incomes (after housing costs)

(b) Recipients of Income Support

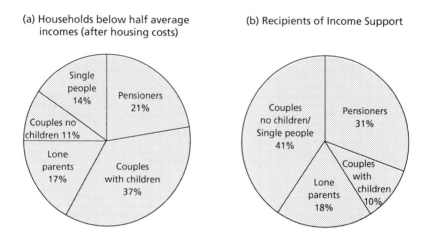

Source: (a) Department of Social Security, *Households below average incomes: a statistical analysis 1979–1992/3. HMSO, 1995;* (b) Department of Social Security, *Social Security statistics.* HMSO, 1995.

More than four out of ten low-income households live in homes rented from a local authority or housing association. But the policy of encouraging home ownership since the early 1980s has resulted in a doubling (to two out of ten) of the proportion of low-income households that are buying a home (Figure 3). Rising homelessness, too, has been a trend over the past 15 years.

Figure 2 Employment

(a) Households below half average
incomes (after housing costs)

(b) Recipients of Income Support

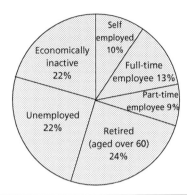

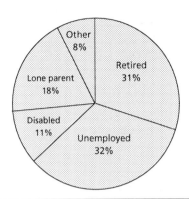

Source: (a) Department of Social Security, *Households below average incomes: a statistical analysis 1979–1992/3.* HMSO, 1995; (b) Department of Social Security, *Social Security statistics.* HMSO, 1995.

Figure 3 Housing

(a) Households below half average
incomes (after housing costs)

(b) Households claiming
Income Support

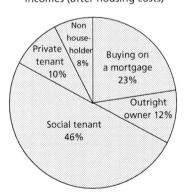

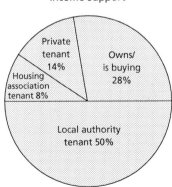

Sources: (a) Department of Social Security, *Households below average incomes: a statistical analysis 1979–1992/3.* HMSO, 1995; (b) Family Resources Survey.

Christine and Alan

Christine and Alan are in their forties and both their children have recently left home. Neither of them is in work: Alan is a painter and decorator and has been out of work for the past two years, while Christine is looking to return to work having been a full-time housewife since their children were born. Their total weekly income from Income Support is £73, which is paid to them once a fortnight. They are buying their home and all but £30 of their £150 a month mortgage repayments are being met by additional social security payments. Their weekly outgoings on bills are £38.04, leaving them £34.96 for food and housekeeping, fares, clothing and personal spending. Christine described their life on benefit as:

> . . . depressing not having any money and when you've got you know a bit to spend you feel . . . I shouldn't really be spending this, I should spend this on food, even if it's your birthday money you know, you shouldn't really be spending it on meself.

> Our treat now, is like getting a box of choc ices at Sainsbury's you know, have a choc ice . . . We don't go pubbing, wouldn't walk in a pub or anything like that.

Christine is a careful money manager and could account for every penny they spent.

> I put it all in envelopes. When I get my giro I get it all in fivers so I can stick it all in the different things you know . . . I've got to put me money away for bills before I can relax and even think about food, I'm just that way inclined . . .

Even so, they had fallen into arrears with both their mortgage and their electricity bills.

Jane

Jane is 28, separated and has two children, James aged six and Alice aged nine. She receives no maintenance from her ex-husband and her total income is £86.12 a week (she has money deducted at source for rent arrears and water rates). Her rent is £51.08 a week but this, like her council tax, is met in full by additional social security payments. Her two children also receive free school meals. Her weekly outgoings are £31.08, leaving her £55.04 a week for all her other outgoings, including food, housekeeping, clothing and spending money. She is a very careful budgeter, writing a list of all the things she needs to get before collecting her benefit Giro.

> *You have to, you can't just go down and think 'Oh I haven't had this for ages, I'll put this in my basket'. You can't do it . . . I try and look for things that are a lot cheaper, because you have to. I'm used to it now, but at first it was awful. I didn't have a clue. You know I was getting my money out on a Monday and by Tuesday I had none. But now I'm pretty good, I'm proud of myself in that respect.*

When she lived with her husband he managed all the bills, but when he moved out he left most of them in arrears. Two years later she is still repaying the rent and council tax arrears. Her husband had been in a relatively well-paid job and she dislikes having to claim benefit since they separated.

> *I suppose I felt alienated because you know I thought 'oh do I have to do this?' But I had to do it for my children's sake. I wasn't bothered about me.*

Jane is a qualified psychiatric nurse and would like to return to work, but the low wages combined with the cost and difficulty of finding childcare prevent her doing so.

Marie

Marie is 48, divorced and living alone since her three children left home. She has been unemployed for almost three years due to ill health. She receives £46.50 a week Income Support, and has all her £47 a week rent and £9.79 council tax paid by additional social security. Her total outgoings are £24.65, leaving her £22.85 for food, cigarettes and all her other outgoings. She has a telephone but had it disconnected to avoid the charges. She collects her benefit fortnightly on Thursday and normally runs short by the Saturday of the second week. She lives in fear of getting into debt and frequently lives on beans on toast to make ends meet.

> You're on the poverty line whichever way you look at it. I get my money on Thursday and I would say by Saturday, I'm broke . . . Nobody can manage on £46 pound a week. You can exist on that. You can't manage it. It goes itself. It can walk out the door in the electric meter and the water rates. You've nothing left to manage with. It is just an existence. It's degrading.

She is looking for a job paying around £140 a week before tax, which she calculates would leave her about £25 a week after meeting all her outgoings so that she could re-establish contact with her friends.

> Because my life is nothing at the moment being unemployed. I can't afford to go out and socialise. I mean you're on the bare necessities and that's exactly what you live in. Going out to work you would meet people and at the end of the day you might just get a social life. Even if it's only one night a week. As it is now its none at all. It's non-existent.

> At the moment, nothing. It's a tunnel . . . it's just black at the moment. If they just found me one glimpse of light . . .

Helen and Stuart

Helen and Stuart are in their late twenties and have four children, the oldest aged five and a half years and the youngest eight weeks. Stuart has been working for seven months but the contract has only one more week to run. Helen is not looking forward to returning to life on Income Support

> *You get your Giro, do your shopping and whatever's left has got to last you two weeks. And when it comes to the middle of the second week, you know, its no money left and you're counting pennies waiting for the next Giro to come in.*

Even while Stuart is in work things have been a struggle.

> *We're in more debt now than we were when he was unemployed. We owe the landlord money, the Council Tax, we owe them money. At least when he was on the dole it was being paid, we didn't have to worry how to find it every week.*

Stuart had been out of work for some time when the temporary job camealong and took it because he was:

> *. . . bored, fed up, sitting around all day, not being able to go out and do anything, it was getting to him.*

He is earning £122 a week after deduc ions and they also receive £45 a week Family Credit and £35.75 a week Child Benefit. Their total weekly income is, therefore, £202.75. They rent from a private landlord paying £93.02 a week rent, £65 of which is covered by Housing Benefit. Their total weekly commitments amount to £71.39, leaving them with £131.36. The following week, when they started claiming Income Support, they would receive a total of £182.80 including Child Benefit. They would almost certainly get their rent and Council Tax met in full so that their commitments would fall to £35.28, leaving them with £147.52 and slightly better off than they are with a low wage.

Note: The reason for their income being greater on Income Support is almost certainly that, when it came for renewal, their Family Credit would have been increased to cover the new baby.

Norman

Norman is a 75-year-old pensioner who, when interviewed, received £63 a week state pension and also had a £5 a week occupational pension. Both his rent (£33.49) and his council tax were met by additional social security payments. His weekly bills came to £16.20, with his electricity charges being the main area of expenditure. He lives in a dark, cold basement but severely restricts his use of electricity for lighting and heating because he is afraid of running up bills he could not afford to pay.

Particularly, when I've got these heaters going in the winter it worries me to death. My kitchen is underground, so I have to turn a light on. I keep thinking about that as well. Same as the bathroom.

After paying his bills he is left with £51.80 a week for food, cigarettes, housekeeping and other expenditure. When money is short he puts food at the bottom of his list

It would be food I guess, certain items of food I would go without.

Over the years he had lowered his expectations and said he was making ends meet:

Quite well on the whole. I manage.

Aims of the study

This report is based on 31 separate studies that were commissioned by the Joseph Rowntree Foundation as part of its social policy and housing research programmes and were completed in 1994 and 1995. In selecting the studies, the emphasis was on those which looked at incomes, major areas of expenditure (such as food, housing, utilities and credit), aspects of household budgeting and the consequences of living on a low income. The report does not, however, attempt to cover health provision, social services or education. (An annotated bibliography of the studies is included in the Appendix.)

Many of the studies focused on households dependent on social security benefits for their income, but about half included people in low-paid jobs and a small number compared life on a low income with the lives of people on average incomes. As a whole, therefore, they span a broad definition of low income – people who live in households with incomes that are below half the national average – and, within this, show how the actual level of income affects people's lives.

Restricting the number of studies in this way created a risk that some topics might not be covered fully (to guard against this, experts were asked to read and comment on draft chapters). But it did mean that the report could become more than just a literature review, with individual pieces of research analysed in depth to provide a detailed insight into the realities of life on a low income. It was, therefore, inappropriate to attribute individual conclusions or quotations to specific studies. In almost all cases the points made in the text are derived from more than one study and the quotations could just as well have been chosen from one study as from another. For that reason, sub-headings have been used liberally and each sub-section referenced at the end.

The value of the approach lies in the fact that the 31 studies combined to provide a remarkably consistent, compelling and wide-ranging picture of life on a low income. Together they draw on detailed accounts given by over 2,100 people of all ages and in a wide range of circumstances, as well as interviews with about 300 people whose work brings them into daily contact with people on low incomes. But despite the large numbers of people interviewed in total, it is important to stress that the evidence remains qualitative. Everyone who participated in the studies was interviewed in depth, and verbatim records were analysed to provide the detailed accounts of their lives. At the same time, many of the studies also included wider statistical analysis and this has been used, along with statistical research for the *Inquiry into Income and Wealth*, to provide background facts and figures. Where these have been quoted they are referenced in the text.

Critics might be tempted to claim that case studies and quotations have been used selectively to present the worst possible picture. Qualitative researchers aim to identify the general pattern that emerges and then to use individual cases as illustrations. Each of the 31 studies was carried out to rigorous standards and was subject to verification by policy makers and others as – indeed, was this report. The fact remains that 31 different research teams, working in different parts of the country on studies with very different aims, have produced results that corroborate each other. The picture that emerges is an uncomfortable one, but it is an accurate reflection of what life is like for poor people in Britain today.

Structure of the report

The report has been structured around two over-arching themes which stand out from the research.

- There is a clear picture of what it means to live on a low income in the mid-1990s and of people's resourcefulness in minimising the impact of having inadequate resources to meet basic needs and decreasing their dependence on public support.

- It is also possible to discern the impact that major changes in social and economic policy over the past 10–15 years have made on the lives of people with low incomes.

Part One of the report focuses on what life is like on a low income in the mid-1990s and comprises three chapters. Chapter 1 begins by looking at how low-income households manage their money and set priorities for spending when money is short. Chapter 2 describes the impact that a low income can have on people's lives, with Chapter 3 exploring how the experience of poverty can vary with people's circumstances.

Part Two shifts the emphasis to specific social and economic policy changes that have affected people living on low incomes. Separate chapters deal with changes in the labour market (Chapter 4); housing policy (Chapter 5); financial services and utilities (Chapter 6); and social security and fiscal policy (Chapter 7). Each considers three main sets of questions: whether policies have made life easier or more difficult for poor people; whether they have helped people to escape poverty or militated against people's efforts to help themselves; and whether they have served to increase or decrease the numbers living on very low incomes.

Part Three brings together the report's conclusions and considers ways in which the quality of life for the poorest people in Britain might be improved. It draws on a discussion of the draft report by researchers, practitioners and policy makers who attended a seminar in December 1995.

PART ONE

1 Making ends meet

Managing money on a low income takes skill; and the poorer people are, the more skill it requires. Not surprisingly some people fail to get it right first time, but far more remarkable is the way that millions of people succeed in managing budgets on incomes that are barely sufficient to cover even the necessities. This chapter explores how people develop their skills in managing money, adapt their patterns of money management and set priorities when faced with a shortfall in their budgets. While many show great resourcefulness, it is clear that, for those living on the very lowest incomes, such strategies are often not enough to make ends meet. They then face the dilemma of being unable to afford essentials such as food, water, fuel and housing.

Developing money management skills

Learning to manage a household budget is a lifetime experience. It usually starts in childhood, is practised in earnest when people set up their own homes and often needs to be revised in response to events in their lives.

When asked how they first learnt to manage money, many adults said they had learnt from their parents – particularly their mothers. Parental influence was strong, especially where they, too, had lived on a low income.

Parents from poor families frequently explained the realities of the family budget to their children at an early age – before they reached their teens. For example, when Susie was widowed she found she could no longer afford to buy her son things when he wanted them. To encourage him to moderate his requests she decided she should talk to him about their financial situation.

> It wasn't long after his father died and I said . . . 'Out of this money I have to pay this and this and this.' I don't believe in telling your children all your business, but he was asking these questions, so I did start saving my receipts from the shop, and I did start presenting him with these bills, and he said 'Oh, mummy how do you manage?'

Because poor children seldom received pocket money, most had to wait until they had an income of their own before they could put what they had learnt into practice. In contrast, children from more middle-class families were less likely to have the family budget explained to them, but were frequently given an allowance when they reached their teens, from which they had to buy their own clothes and meet other expenses. This gave them an opportunity to learn at first-hand how to manage their own budget.

In most cases, though, it was not until they left home that people had to manage a household budget for themselves. For those whose parents had been careful money managers, it usually involved emulating tried and tested methods. But for others it was a matter of evolving a method through trial and error – often making mistakes. This was especially the case for people who adopted a pay-as-you-go approach.

Many people lived on low incomes for most, if not all, of their lives and, while they found things hard when they were young, the more practice they had, the better they got at managing their money.

> I don't have any more money than I used to when I started on benefit, it's just that now I know what I can and cannot do.

A couple in their mid-forties, summed up this gradual learning process when they attributed their skills to:

> . . . 20 years' experience. We've been together 20 years. You have to learn the hard way sometimes. As the years go by you learn . . . you make mistakes and you learn by them.

Things were even more difficult for people who were suddenly confronted with having to manage on a low income – either because they lost their jobs or because they had become divorced or widowed, especially if their partner had previously managed the household budget. For these people it was a matter of having to adapt quickly with little room for making mistakes. Bill-juggling or using credit to pay bills was a common response to outgoings that exceeded income, largely because people did not expect to remain on a low income for long and saw it as a way of tiding them over.

People who had lost jobs often believed that they would soon find work again and, while it is easy to criticise this lack of prudence, the belief was an important part of the confidence needed to overcome the difficulties of finding another job. But bill-juggling could not be sustained in the long-term. If they remained on a low income, most people eventually found ways of getting their situation under control. A couple who had enjoyed spending money when the husband was in work, described how they had adjusted to living on benefit.

At one time we used to get his Giro on a Saturday, and Saturday night we hadn't got two pennies to rub together. And then you've got to go like a fortnight before you've got any money. But gradually, over the years, you tend to think, 'Well, no, I need to pay so and so, and so and so'.

In another case, a lone mother, who had been relatively well-off before her divorce, was surprised at how she had adapted to life on a low income.

It does, you know, become a way of life not having any money all the time. I never thought I would live like this, watching the pennies, but I do because I have to.

This process of 'learning by doing' seems to be an important reason why older people, as a rule, avoid getting into financial difficulties. Certainly they generally have a careful approach to money management, which is often attributed to a strong aversion among the older generation to owing money. Yet a study of water debt found that attitudes to bill-paying did not offer an adequate explanation for older people being more likely than others to keep up to date with their water bills. Even when income, family circumstances and attitudes were controlled, age was still a highly significant factor explaining water debt. Experience and practice seemed to be more important than attitudes.

(Dobson *et al*, 1994; Herbert and Kempson, 1995; Kempson *et al*, 1994; Middleton *et al*, 1994; Morris and Ritchie, 1994; Speak *et al*, 1995.)

Patterns of money management

Women bear the brunt of managing low incomes. Three out of ten low-income households are headed by lone mothers or widowed pensioners. Even among couples, who account for six out of ten low-income households, the research shows that the woman is very likely to both control and manage the household budget. Occasionally this was because the man had abdicated responsibility for what seemed to him to be a thankless task. More commonly it was a way of ensuring tight control over the budget, with women considered the more careful money managers.

(Kempson *et al*, 1994; Morris and Ritchie, 1994.)

Approaches to money management
Rich or poor, people differ in their approaches to money management. Some keep a close watch on their money, while others tend to muddle through from one pay-day to the next. Some try to save when they can, others enjoy spending.

But the evidence suggests that there is not a simple dichotomy between careful savers and spendthrift muddlers – at least not among people on low incomes. Moreover, as we have seen, people changed their approach to money management in response to changes in their circumstances.

A study of 74 low-income families with children found that about two-thirds of households were careful with their money, with most of them planning their spending in detail. In some instances this involved writing down and costing a budget for the week, as described by Marion, a lone mother living with her four children on Income Support.

> *I have to write everything out before I get paid. I write absolutely everything that I've got to buy, you know, for the week . . . I write everything down to the last tee and that's how I manage.*

Some people who operated cash budgets physically allocated money to different purposes once it had been received. Envelopes, jars and boxes were used – even among those who, in the past had been accustomed to writing cheques and paying bills on standing order. Mark and Debbie, who started claiming Income Support after Mark lost his job, developed a system using envelopes to ensure that all their bills were covered and that they knew how much would be left over for food and other shopping.

> *Out of every Giro we get now it is all segregated into what we're going to have for the gas, what goes into there . . . and just have what's left . . . We normally try and budget ourselves out to what we expect the bill to be and then, if it's over what we budgeted, we've still got that month then to make up the balance, which hasn't been a vast amount. We haven't been caught short.*

Others kept detailed records of what they had spent, but did not really plan their spending in advance. As a strategy this was much less successful and often associated with financial difficulties. It was usually adopted by people who recognised that they had spending tendencies they needed to control or who were trying to be more careful since falling into arrears with their bills.

About a third of the households used a pay-as-you-go approach, neither planning ahead nor recording their spending. A few had always managed their money that way and admitted they lacked money management skills. Others found that, while they had been careful with money when there was enough to go round, their management system broke down when money was tight. Bill-juggling, or 'robbing Peter to pay Paul', was common in these households and frequently led to arrears.

We've tried [budgeting] different ways, but it still comes out the same. You do the best you can . . . We try to sort out the bills as they come in. Rob Peter to pay Paul – that's what you have to do. Then try and catch up on everybody. Every week . . . you look at the bills and work it out . . . you can never get it all together. I'm going to have to miss the electricity this week to pay something else.

People who operated a pay-as-you-go system of money management were not always the ones with spending tendencies. Some, like the couple above, had saved when times were better. Others had taken steps to curb their spending tendencies. They made sure that bills were always paid as soon as they received their money, using standing orders, payment plans and pre-payment meters to avoid the temptation of spending the money on other things.

As I get [my benefit] on a Monday, I go straight over and get the [electricity] cards. Everything is dealt with on a Monday, 'cos if it's left in a jar, or something, you'd be dipping in for this and for that and nothing would ever get paid.

I get these [benefits] on a Monday and they go straight into the bank and there's standing orders for everything. If I didn't do that then I would be [in financial difficulties]. I'm a spendthrift, I would spend all of it.

(Kempson *et al*, 1994.)

Current accounts and cash budgets
About half of households living on a low income had a current bank or building society account with the remainder operating a cash budget – largely as a matter of choice. When money was tight, people were worried about bank charges and, in any case, preferred the control that a cash budget gave them. This had deterred some from ever having an account but, more commonly, they had either suspended use of their current account or closed it down altogether. It is, therefore, not surprising to find that there was a strong association between cash budgets and living on benefit.

(Kempson *et al*, 1994.)

Setting priorities

Managing on a low income involves more than keeping a close eye on what is spent. In all cases it is also a matter of setting priorities for spending – and the poorer people are the more difficult are the choices. The room for manoeuvre is small and most find themselves having to either cut back on essentials, such as food and fuel, or falling behind with their bills.

Cutting out 'luxuries'

There are some areas of expenditure that just about all households living on a low income cut back because they are considered 'luxuries': social activities, 'treats', and decorating and repairs are usually the first to go.

Holidays tended to be a thing of the past for anyone who had lived on a low income for any length of time, even though many felt that getting away even for a few days would relieve the strain on their family. Where parents could afford it, day trips were substituted for 'proper holidays', with school outings offering a way of giving the children a break without incurring the cost of adult fares. When asked about her holidays over the past year, Nicola, a 7-year-old girl from a poor family, said she had visited:

Nicola: Southport – it's a trip what I go on. Sometimes they take you to Skegness but, when you went, you had to get up right early to get the coach.

Interviewer: How long did you stay?

Nicola: The whole day.

Contrast her replies with those of 11-year-old Samantha, who was from a middle-class family.

Samantha: France at Easter with Grandma and Granddad.

Interviewer: Have you been there before?

Samantha: Yes, we go there every year, twice a year. And then we go and stay with our other grandparents at bank holidays in England and with my aunt and uncle or we stay in hotels. At Christmas we stay at home. We go to other places on day trips. We go away for a long time in the big holidays, like summer.

Interviewer: Where?

Samantha: Africa.

Managing on a low income imposed other social restrictions. Adults could not afford an evening out or to invite friends for a meal. Because most of their friends were in the same financial position, they received few invitations to meals and often turned them down because they could not return the hospitality. In the absence of a social life, watching television (and in some cases videos) was an important activity.

Children living in low-income families also experienced a more restricted social life than their peers (with the notable exception of only children of lone mothers, who were worried about becoming socially isolated). Outside school, poor children were much less likely to participate in music, dance or drama classes, to play sports (other than football) or to be member of clubs such as Cubs/Scouts or Brownies/Guides. They also had fewer opportunities to invite friends to their homes for meals.

A further area selected for cutbacks was what was generally termed 'treats'. This usually referred to foodstuffs such as cakes and biscuits, more expensive fresh fruits, wine, and take-away meals. It also included foods with a cultural significance – a 'proper Sunday lunch' or, for some Afro-Caribbean families, buying Caribbean foods.

Decorating and repairs were also, almost universally, regarded as non-essential expenditure. As a consequence, people not only spent much of their lives at home but often did so in surroundings that were rather depressing – in need of redecorating, lacking floor coverings and inadequately furnished. People setting up home on low incomes, young single mothers in particular, often lived in very basic homes.

(Dobson *et al*, 1994; Grant, 1995; Kempson *et al*, 1994; Middleton *et al*, 1994; Morris and Ritchie, 1994; Speak *et al*, 1995.)

Other non-essentials

Debates about living on a low income invariably come round to whether scarce money is wasted on drinking, smoking and gambling. But what is the evidence?

A study of single homeless people found that homelessness and drinking 'went hand in hand'. Although whether excessive drinking was the consequence of, or a cause of, homelessness was by no means clear.

> . . . *whether you drink 'cos you're homeless or whether you're homeless because you drink, it's two ways. It's a Catch 22 situation. You can drink 'cos you're homeless looking for company; 'cos you get fed up of sitting in the hostel seeing the same old faces, and then when you start drinking you go through your money . . . so you finish up on the streets.*

In general, though, the research shows that drinking alcohol (including both visits to the pub and bottles of wine with a meal) was considered a luxury by people on low incomes and was one of the first areas of expenditure to be cut. This is consistent with the government's *Family Expenditure Survey*, which shows that alcohol consumption falls with declining income levels. However, expenditure on tobacco increases.

In fact, smoking was also often considered a luxury by people on low incomes, but they often cut down rather than give up altogether. People who would have described themselves as '20 a day' smokers, for example, tended to smoke fewer cigarettes towards the end of the week as they ran short of money. Often they bought fewer still as friends would offer them cigarettes when they had run out.

Most smokers were aware that it meant they had less money, but could not face adding to their problems by trying to give up smoking. They led stressful lives and smoking was the only was they reduced the stress, while people with more money went out for the evening, took holidays or sat down with a drink at the end of the day.

If my circumstances improved and I had less worry, I'd smoke less.

The kids know that when I sit down to have a fag, they're not to bother me. When I do this, it means that I'm not in and I've gone out and they have to sort themselves out until I've finished. That probably sounds awful, but I don't go out and I'm always with the kids. You can see for yourself that there's not much room here and I can't really leave them on their own, so this is what I do. I would rather be hungry than not have any fags.

Many adults did go without food to pay for their cigarettes, although the parents among them did not allow it to affect spending on their children. So, while low-income smokers had poorer diets than non-smokers, there was no difference in the diets of their children.

Queues to buy National Lottery tickets have added to the list of criticisms that poor people are wasting money when they cannot afford to pay their bills. The lottery was introduced after most of the research considered in this report was complete, and it is not known whether people buy lottery tickets with money that is needed for food or bills. But there is no shortage of insights into why they might be tempted to divert money to playing the lottery. Many people living on a low income could see no prospect of their situation improving 'unless we win the pools'.

(Dobson *et al*, 1994; Dowler and Calvert, 1995; Kempson *et al*, 1994; Speak *et al*, 1995.)

Saving money on essentials

Having cut out what they regarded as luxuries, most people try to save money on essentials, like food and clothing, by either cutting back or buying cheap goods.

Food

Food accounts for a very high proportion of the spending by people living on low incomes and is frequently the area of the budget offering greatest flexibility. Moreover, as the research showed, food shopping was an area where women were particularly resourceful.

Where they had a choice of high street supermarkets, street markets and specialist shops, they shopped around looking for bargains and value for money. But this was time-consuming and while it was seen as a challenge by some:

> There's always special offers and that so you can easily save quite a bit by shopping around. There is a difference between shops on things like coffee and that, so it makes sense. It took me quite a while to realise how much of a difference, though.

it was a necessary chore for others:

> You do notice a difference between things in the different shops and it's worth going back to get it if it's cheaper. Pennies make a difference to me. I would much rather go to one shop and get everything done in one go, but I can't afford it so there's no point in complaining about it.

Not only were the large supermarkets more expensive than discount stores and street markets but, with the growing trend of out-of-town shopping, they were impossible to reach for people who did not have access to private transport.

In addition to shopping around, many women shopped at the end of the day, when bargains could be found. Doing this could save several pounds on staple foods.

If you go down [to the market] just before they pack up, they are giving the fruit away. They don't want to take it home with them, so they sell it cheap . . . It's the same with your bread in the supermarkets. When they are closing they are reducing the bread and . . . you can get loaves for 25p.

Generally speaking, women took sole responsibility for the shopping and usually found it easier to go shopping alone. This was partly because of the saving on bus fares, but also because they tended to spend more money when their partners or children accompanied them.

The normal pattern was to do the 'main shop' on benefit or pay-day and to supplement it by buying items like bread and milk during the week. Those who received their benefit payments fortnightly tended to spend more in the first week than they did in the second.

Weekly shopping was preferred to the monthly pattern that was more common in better-off households, because it gave more control. Having food in the store cupboard or fridge created a risk that partners and older children would help themselves, making it difficult to ration food over a fortnight. Indeed, where money was unusually scarce, women resorted to buying only what would be eaten that day. Such frequent shopping trips were, however, a matter of necessity, not choice.

> I used to be able just to go and shop for a couple of weeks which was great. It was over and done with and you didn't have to worry . . . Now I get most of what I need for the week then I still have to go out and get the bread and things every day. It's the routine that's so awful – I'm in the shops every day even if it's just for milk and that.

Women often ran a systematic variation in their weekly shopping, with different things being bought on alternate weeks. This enabled them to buy in larger quantities, which tended to be cheaper, and to take advantage of discounts linked to 'multi-buys'.

There is, however, a danger of painting too rosy a picture of women's resourcefulness that ignores the strain that it placed on many of them. Most of the time they simply got on with the task of stretching the food budget as far as they could. But occasionally they stopped to compare themselves with other shoppers or to reflect on times when money had been less scarce.

> When you're pushing the trolley around and you see people pushing one that's almost full and yours isn't, I think 'I wish I could just put what I wanted in and not have to worry', but I can't.

> I would like a day out to go shopping – just for food – to have the money and not get to the till and have to put things back. Not being used to it, it got harder and harder each week. It's not that I don't like shopping. I hate it.

(Dobson *et al*, 1994; Dowler and Calvert, 1995; Kempson *et al*, 1994; Middleton *et al*, 1994; Speak *et al*, 1995.)

Clothes
Clothing is the other main area where economies are made. Adults interviewed for the research usually bought themselves second-hand clothes, from charity shops or jumble sales, or they made do or mended what they had got. New clothes were a rarity. But when it came to clothing their children, few parents were prepared to compromise. Children did not like receiving either 'hand-ons' or second-hand clothes and would only wear them under protest. They feared rejection by their friends for being 'poor', and their parents wanted to protect them from this stigma.

As a consequence, parents needed to shop around for their children's clothing and footwear, comparing prices and quality in the discount shops, street markets and mail-order catalogues. Mothers were concerned to buy the best quality clothes and shoes they could afford and mail-order catalogues were popular, as they offered a way of buying better quality new things and spreading the cost across the year. Buying very cheap and poorly made goods from markets or some discount stores was considered a false economy, especially if there were younger children to whom they could be handed on. There were, however, two situations when this did not apply – the need to buy something unexpectedly and clothing for young boys who were 'heavy' on clothes and shoes.

Mothers also tried to ensure that clothing lasted as long as possible by buying it a size or two too large. This was particularly the case for larger items of expenditure, such as winter coats. Sales were a good source of cheap but high-quality clothing, which could be 'bought big' and kept for the next season.

(Kempson *et al*, 1994; Middleton *et al*, 1994.)

Making difficult choices

Despite these efforts to economise, some people were still unable to make ends meet. This was usually the case where people lived on very low earnings or Income Support. They then faced some hard choices, to which two main approaches can be identified:

* going without essentials to pay bills and avoid having to use credit

* juggling bills and using credit to avoid going without essentials.

People employing the first of these approaches went without food and fuel to tide themselves over until they received their next payment of benefit or wages. This meant missing meals or living on toast; going to bed very early in winter or sitting in the cold with blankets; and even living in the dark because there was no money for tokens to feed the electricity meter.

The second approach created a constant cycle of delaying bill payments or borrowing to pay them, both of which merely put off the day when payment had to be made. People in this situation regularly found themselves being chased by creditors.

It is tempting to ascribe these quite distinct approaches to fundamental differences in people's value systems. And, up to a point, this was true. Some people put their creditors before their family, paying their bills as soon as they received their wages or benefit and then eking out what money was left.

> *It's many times, come to Saturday, we run out of money (for bread and milk) of a weekend. That's hard luck, because you've got to wait 'til Monday. Simple as that . . . We can survive without them. It won't kill us.*

Others believed that large companies could wait and their families came first.

> *If I know we ain't got no food and the gas man's waiting, I'm sorry, I'm going to buy my shopping. They're OK. The gas will survive.*

Nevertheless, family circumstances and the length of time people had lived on a low income seemed to be more important factors than any long-held principles or values.

Going without essentials was easier when adults had only themselves to consider, but far more difficult when it meant denying others – especially children. The research shows a larger proportion of pensioner households deciding to go without than was the case among families with children.

Bill-juggling was most common when people first had to manage on a low income. This included young people setting up home on their own who were learning money management 'on the job' through a process of trial and error. It was also common among people who had recently experienced a large drop in income. They may have been fairly careful money managers in the past but, having lost their jobs or separated from a partner, they found it impossible to meet their commitments on a greatly reduced income.

Bill-juggling was not, however, a sustainable strategy and was much less common among those who had lived on very low incomes for any length of time. There were two main reasons for this. First they learnt from experience. For example, Angela, who had learnt how to manage her money over the past 20 years, described how, at a time when they had no money to pay their bills, she sat down to think through where she had gone wrong. Secondly, once people fell into arrears, creditors persuaded (or forced) them to pay their bills in ways that gave them little room for juggling. These included the installation of pre-payment meters for fuel and water or direct deductions from benefit to cover fuel, water, rent or council tax.

(Dobson *et al*, 1994; Kempson *et al*, 1994; Morris and Ritchie 1994; Speak *et al*, 1995).

Dynamics of making ends meet

In fact, just about everyone living on a very low income had difficulty managing from one week to the next and unexpected expenditure disrupted even the most carefully planned budget. A study of 74 low-income families with children showed that only a minority (12) had managed to keep their heads above water over the past year and seemed likely to remain that way over the coming one. Following the analogy through, the report allocated the families to one of four groups:

- 32 families who were keeping their heads above water

- 6 families who had been making ends meet but were sinking into financial difficulty and falling into arrears with bills

- 16 families who had arrears on a number of commitments, but were struggling to the surface and recovering their difficulties

- 20 families who seemed to be drowning in financial problems. They described themselves as struggling to make ends meet, had been in arrears with various household bills for some time and saw no prospect of things getting any easier.

Over a period of two years most families moved from one group to another and the labels 'feckless' and 'respectable' poor had little relevance.

Figure 4 Changes over time

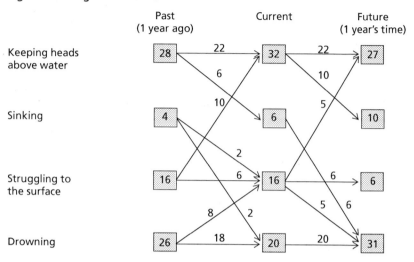

	Past (1 year ago)	Current	Future (1 year's time)

Keeping heads above water: 28, 32, 27
Sinking: 4, 6, 10
Struggling to the surface: 16, 16, 6
Drowning: 26, 20, 31

It seemed that the outcome for families depended on a number of distinct (but not necessarily unrelated) factors: the income and other resources they had; how they used those resources; their family circumstances; and the steps they took to make ends meet. These are all explored in greater detail in Chapter 3.

(Kempson *et al*, 1994.)

Summary

People who cannot make ends meet are sometimes accused of being either feckless or poor money managers. But, while some people manage to balance their budgets more successfully than others, the evidence for fecklessness is scant. Some start out better able to manage their budgets than others – often because they had learnt from parents who were also poor. But there is strong evidence that, over time, people become more knowledgeable and practised at managing a low-income budget.

Most people living on low incomes adjust their patterns of money management, bill-paying and shopping to a point where managing the household budget becomes almost a full-time occupation. Certainly it preoccupies the minds of most women most of the time. Faced with the need to make ends meet they first cut out 'luxuries', even though these are things that most people would take for granted. If that proves insufficient, they pare back spending on essentials like food and clothing. And if that is not enough, as is often the case in households dependent on benefit, they have to make some very difficult choices in order to make ends meet.

In fact, as the research shows, people generally exercise tremendous control over their spending wherever they can. Yet, as later chapters make clear, they had little control over the things that would really have made a difference to their standard of living: job markets, wage rates, benefit levels, costs of housing, fuel and other essentials. Looking after the pennies did not necessarily mean that the pounds would look after themselves.

2 Life on a low income

There is no clear point at which people can be said to live in poverty; it is a matter of degree. The poorer people are, the more difficult it becomes to make ends meet, with the very poorest finding it difficult to cover even the necessities, such as food, heating and a roof over their heads. Real poverty still exists in Britain.

As highlighted in the previous chapter, there is a hierarchy of approaches to living on a low income. Those with modest incomes restrict their social lives and cut out 'luxuries'. On a lower income, people try to cut back spending on essentials; while those on the very lowest incomes face either going without food and fuel or getting into debt. As a consequence the struggle to make ends meet not only affects family life, but can result in poor diet, lack of fuel and water, poor housing and homelessness, debt, poor physical health, and stress and mental health problems. The poorer people are, the more likely they are to experience these problems.

Impact on family life

Many people found that they lost contact with their friends, especially as their financial difficulties increased and they could neither afford to go out nor invite friends to their home for a meal. In some cases, people cut themselves off because they could not face socialising. Where friends were in the same financial position, it was especially depressing to get together as the conversation inevitably came round to money matters. Mixing with better-off friends also had its drawbacks.

> *I have lost all my friends. I don't go out much now, but a few years ago when I used to go and see my friends, as soon as they saw me the first thing that struck them was maybe I was coming to borrow something. Even if I had come to say 'Hello'.*

As a consequence low-income families spent a good deal of time in one another's company, especially when no-one went out to work. This could cement strong relationships but, more often, it placed a strain on them.

Little things that never mattered before are suddenly major issues and you fight over them. I fight with him [her husband], I shout at the kids, he does as well and the kids cry. They probably don't argue any more than they used to, but because we're here all the time it seems like it.

Constant money problems led to turbulent personal relationships and, for some, separation and divorce. In extreme cases constant arguments about money resulted in physical violence.

Family arguments were often the reason why young people from low-income families left home. For example, Janice had a stormy relationship with her mother and walked out after one particularly bad row.

When I say arguing, it wasnae shouting and bawling, it was like battering each other and kicking lumps off each other – that sort of thing. And she just told me to go and I wasnae going to stay wi' her going on like that . . . I just put everything, all my clothes in a big red bin bag . . . and I took that from place to place . . . I went to a friend's place and stayed there for a while, then just kept kind of moving on.

As in Janice's case, this frequently led to homelessness as the move out was generally unplanned and parents were unlikely to offer either emotional or financial support.

In much the same way, living on a low income could strengthen ties within extended families or it could set up strains. Mother and daughter relationships were frequently very strong as they helped one another out both financially and emotionally. Occasionally, though, lack of money drove a wedge in family relationships. Most commonly this occurred when people could not repay the money they had borrowed, but there were also instances where people could not afford to fulfil family obligations. For example, one young woman had been very upset at the criticism she received from her brothers and sisters when she could not afford to buy a wreath for her father's funeral.

(Dobson *et al*, 1994; Grant, 1995; Herbert and Kempson, 1996; Jones, 1995; Kempson *et al*, 1994; Speak *et al*, 1995.)

Poor diet

Food choices and levels of expenditure on food are normally constrained within low-income households. As already seen, when households are operating on very tight budgets, spending on food is often the main area of flexibility.

In general people living on very low incomes had poorer diets than those who were better off – with low dietary variety and inadequate nutrient intakes. Only rarely was it through complete ignorance. Certainly some very young single mothers had limited cooking skills when they set up home on their own, but there was little evidence that people were unaware of what constituted a healthy diet. Most were only too aware that they had unhealthy diets, but put them down to lack of money.

> When I was living with his [her son's] father, I just ate better. I had better quality food. That's something that's really changed. I find increasingly that I can't afford to buy fresh fruit and vegetables.

> We try to eat 'proper' meals like meat and veg and that, but there isn't the money to do it all the time. So we eat properly once or twice a week, depending on the money, and the rest of the time we make do with things like sausages, pies, potatoes and things like beans. The meals aren't as good but they do the job, they'll fill them up and stop them from being hungry. It's the best I can do.

> The kids live on things like fish fingers and, you know, the convenience foods that are really cheap to buy in bulk and if I had more money I would feed them differently. They seem healthy enough, but my conscience is pricked all the time because I feel I'm not doing the best for them.

In fact diets deteriorated over the period from benefit collection day. This was shown by studies of nutritional intake and acknowledged by people themselves, who regularly spoke of having to make do with whatever they could find in the store cupboard or fridge at the end of the week.

> I improvise. One week I had only milk and flour, so I made milk buns; they really filled us up.

> Well, basically I just have to mix and match what I've got together in the cupboard and cook it up.

(Dobson *et al*, 1994; Dowler and Calvert, 1995.)

School meals

Many mothers living on Income Support appreciated the fact that their children received free school meals. It was one meal less to worry about.

I know they don't think that much of them, but at least I know that they're getting something hot. Knowing my lot, they'll be eating the chips and that but at least they're eating. Do you know, there's been times when that was the only meal they had, 'cos when they'd come home there just wasn't the money so they'd eat bread or cereal, anything to fill them up. Thank God that hasn't happened in a while, but at least if you know that they've had something hot you don't need to feel so bad.

Detailed investigation of the meals eaten by low-income families showed that school meals were often far from healthy, just as this mother suspected. Children often ate the cheap convenience food that parents worried about having to give them themselves. Those who were given packed lunches often had a more varied and healthy meal. The box below contrasts the lunches eaten by the teenage children of two lone parent families.

School lunches
Eaten by the teenage children of a lone mother living on Income Support.

Becky   Pastie, orange drink, apple crumble and custard
Paula   Chicken nuggets, beetroot, bubble gum drink, cake and custard
Alan   Chicken nuggets, spaghetti, chips and cake

Packed lunches
Eaten by the teenage children of a lone mother in work.

Helen   Edam cheese sandwich with pickle, red pepper salad with salad cream, sponge cake, peanuts, raisins, apple, Ribena
Simon   Edam cheese sandwich with pickle, Twiglets, peanuts, raisins, apple, Ribena

Source: Dowler and Calvert, 1995.

That school meals fail to address the dietary problems of children from poor families must surely be a matter of concern.

(Dobson *et al*, 1994; Dowler and Calvert, 1995.)

Achieving a healthy diet

Although there are clear links between low income and nutritional deprivation, it is only part of the explanation. Some people on low incomes achieve healthier diets than others and it seems likely that attitudes towards shopping, cooking and eating may lead to these variations.

When faced with the need to cut back on spending, the people interviewed differed in the relative importance they assigned to the quantity and quality of the food their families ate. Some bought cheaper, poorer quality foods, while others simply ate less.

Many women, especially those with children, wanted to avoid waste and so tended to buy foods that they knew the whole family would eat. This often led to a diet with a regular weekly pattern in which cooking and meal planning became a chore.

There were, however, other women for whom preparing healthy meals on a low income was a challenge. Lone mothers on Income Support who looked for 'fresh', 'healthy' foods, by shopping around different food outlets, achieved diets which were of a much higher nutritional standard than the mothers whose primary considerations were to buy food that was 'cheap' or would not be wasted. Even so, they could only overcome some of the disadvantages of a low income. Among people who looked for healthy food, those who were poor achieved less healthy diets than those who were better off.

Moreover, some women were restricted in their efforts to buy healthy food by the lack of fresh food outlets in their neighbourhood.

(Dobson *et al*, 1994; Dowler and Calvert, 1995; Grant 1995; Kempson *et al*, 1994; Speak *et al*, 1995.)

Restricted use of fuel and water

Heating

Most people were cautious about their use of heating, with interviewers often reporting that, in winter, homes were bitterly cold. Individual rooms were heated as needed – normally during the coldest part of the late evening. Central heating, even where it was available, was not used. For people who were at home all day, the costs of heating their homes was of particular concern – especially if they needed to stay warm either for health reasons or because they had young children.

Although levels of gas and electricity disconnection are not high, they tend to be heavily concentrated among low-income households. And it was often the fear of disconnection that led to rationing of use. Ivy, for example, was 75 years old and suffered from chronic asthma which meant that she was not very active and spent most of her time at home. She was living on a basic pension, supplemented by a modest occupational pension of £76 a month, and did not want to run the risk of fuel bills she could not afford.

This time last year, February, I was really down. I were going without heating. I had me coat on, I had a thick coat on, cardigans, socks. I daren't have the heating on . . .

While pre-payment meters undoubtedly helped some people to spread the cost of fuel bills, charges were higher for gas and electricity bought in that way. People who were repaying fuel bill arrears through their pre-payment meter faced additional problems, as they were recouped by an adjustment to the tariff they paid. This meant that the more fuel they used, the more of their arrears they were repaying.

Pre-payment meters reinforced people's awareness of their fuel consumption, encouraging the tendency towards rationing use.

Sometimes, when the meter goes I have to press the emergency or go and borrow – it's a special button. If your money runs out you can press that and get £2 and you have to pay the meter back . . . I keep on going and having a look at the meter to see how much is on the meter and pray someone brings some money in time, 'cos you can't press it again. 'Cos it will not give you again until you pay it back.

I try to cut down on me electric. Many a Sunday afternoon our electric has gone. We've just waited 'til Monday [the day she collected her benefit].

This was such a regular occurrence for this lone mother that she had strategies for coping without mains electricity: she used a camping light and wired their television up to a car battery when the meter ran out.

(Grant, 1995; Kempson *et al*, 1994; Morris and Ritchie, 1994; Speak *et al*, 1995.)

Water
Until relatively recently, water charges were low and often paid with council rents. So, unlike fuel bills, they did not cause any particular problems. But rising water bills, and the advent of both metered use and pre-payment devices, have led to situations not unlike those faced for gas and electricity.

About 7 per cent of households currently have their water supply metered and are, therefore, charged according to the amount of water they use. While there is no coercion for people to pay this way, new homes are now being fitted with meters as a matter of routine. This creates a dilemma for people who, having waited for rehousing, are offered a new home.

For example, Samira and her youngest child had lived with one of her adult sons since her husband had died. This was both overcrowded and difficult as her five year old had cerebral palsy and most of the house was inaccessible to wheelchair use. She had waited some time for suitable rehousing and was offered a new bungalow by a housing association. But the water supply was metered and she was worried about the high costs she would incur, because her child's disabilities meant he generated a great deal of washing. There is growing evidence that poor families who have metered water supplies ration their use for essentials such as washing and flushing the toilet.

Water disconnections tend to be concentrated among low-income households. This has led some water companies to experiment with pre-payment meters, although, unlike their gas and electricity counterparts, charges are not linked to use – the meters simply spread the cost of annual water bills. With the safeguard of emergency supply 'on credit', a water supply is assured as long as the meter has been charged up. Like pre-payment fuel meters, these water budgeting devices are often welcomed by poor people, but they also run the risk of people disconnecting themselves because they can not afford to feed the meter.

> *If you forget to fill up you will be disconnected and that will be it. It doesn't mess about, that machine, it will cut you off whatever you do.*

(Grant, 1995; Herbert and Kempson, 1995.)

Debt

Low-income households frequently fall behind with their bills and being in debt affects their lives in a number of ways. Most feel a sense of shame and the unsympathetic debt recovery practices of some creditors cause added anxiety. A minority end up in court, losing their homes or having their fuel or water supply disconnected.

Stigma of poverty and debt

Many people spoke of the stigma of being poor: of being conscious that the food they had in their supermarket trolleys was different from other shoppers; of the embarrassment of getting to the checkout only to find they did not have enough money for the bill; of never having decent clothing; of not being able to afford presents for others; and of having a home to which they felt ashamed to invite others.

But the shame of being in debt was felt most of all.

You feel degraded. You think other people know that you are in debt. You think you have done something wrong.

When they turned the water tap off, I felt very upset, I can't explain . . . I feel very ashamed at that time. I feel personally ashamed. I feel ashamed at myself. I couldn't manage to pay the water and the supply had been cut off.

This shame became very public for people who had their homes repossessed as a result of mortgage arrears. The majority of them spoke of the 'shame', 'lost pride' and 'lost respect' they felt when they had to face their family and friends.

(Dobson *et al*, 1994; Grant, 1995; Ford, 1994; Herbert and Kempson, 1995; Kempson *et al*, 1994; Morris and Ritchie, 1994; Speak *et al*, 1995.)

Debt recovery practices
The links between low income and debt are well established. A high proportion of people who fall behind with their commitments either live on very low incomes or have experienced a sudden drop in income, generally through job loss or relationship breakdown. The great majority of people in these circumstances acknowledge that they owe the money and feel under an obligation to pay their creditors. In other words it is a question of 'can't pay' and not 'won't pay'.

These basic facts do not seem, however, to have been accepted by some creditors. People in debt encountered little sympathy when they contacted their creditors to explain their difficulties and try to negotiate a way of paying what they owed.

Several phone calls and letters were exchanged. I tried to explain the position, basically they didn't want to know. (Mortgage arrears following job loss)

I went to see them . . . He was a very abrupt person. He didn't want to listen to reason. He didn't want to know my circumstances. I said to him 'I can afford to pay (I think it was) £10 a week'. And he said 'Well that's just not good enough' . . . He just dismissed it. We're not accepting it, end of story. (Poll tax arrears following long-term sickness)

I just think they should listen if you are in financial difficulties and you're trying to say 'Look I'm not avoiding paying it, I just can't pay what you're asking, but I will pay this.' (Water debt following a relationship breakdown, leaving the wife with unpaid bills and facing repossession)

There were instances of creditors using fairly aggressive methods of debt recovery that were inappropriate under the circumstances. John, for example, had his water supply disconnected, despite having notified the water company that he had moved out of his home following a nervous breakdown which led to him being off work. He also suffered from Repetitive Strain Injury.

I've written letters to them saying that this is my situation, that I will be disabled . . . [and asking] 'What can you suggest for me to do?' And I received a letter back saying that they're going to take me to court 'cos I've not paid and I explained to them about that. 'I can't afford to pay, please help me, have you got any suggestions?' And then I got another letter back saying 'You have got to pay this money, we're still taking you to court'.

There were even instances bordering on harassment.

They continually wrote. I was in a right state . . . They'd ring me up four or five times a day. We had a terrible time, honestly. Just constantly ringing.

Valerie had only just been discharged from hospital when a creditor turned up on her doorstep.

This particular man came to the house before it actually went to court. I'd come out of hospital the one day and he came the next. I was in a terrible state because I'd had me chest operated on and I were all stitched up here. I was in a bit of a mess and a lot of pain and he came and he was so arrogant.'You're living a life of luxury here. I'm not having this. There's no reason why you can't pay more. You've got a better standard of living than I've got.' Oh! and he reduced me to tears, which is not really like me. It's getting more and more like me as time goes by.

Such heartless harassment was by no means usual, but it was a good deal more commonplace than might have been expected.

(Ford, 1994; Grant, 1995; Herbert and Kempson, 1995; Kempson *et al*, 1994;

Morris and Ritchie 1994; Speak *et al*, 1995).

Disconnection and repossession

In the main, poor people's debts are for basic household bills – rent, mortgage, gas, electricity, water and Council Tax. This is in contrast to better-off debtors where arrears on consumer credit are much more common. The types of debt incurred by poor people are, therefore, the ones that carry the harshest sanctions: repossession, disconnection and, in the case of local taxes, imprisonment. The experiences of people who have been through these sanctions are frequently disturbing.

About half of the 12,500 water disconnections a year are for more than 24 hours. Rachel and Steve, for example, were disconnected for three weeks before they could get together the money to be reconnected. During this time:

We went round to the next-door neighbours and filled up the bath with water through their hose and used that for washing, toilet, food and that sort of thing . . . I was very worried and concerned as the main problem is health . . . the main problem is keeping yourself clean by washing and the toilet . . . basically I just thought they were putting my health at risk.

Most people whose water was disconnected relied on neighbours in this way. Others moved out of their homes until they had their supply restored and some survived using bottled water for drinking and collecting rainwater for all other purposes.

Fears about becoming homeless worried people facing possession proceedings for mortgage arrears. It was common for people to have no idea where they would live until the very last moment.

I went four months before we actually lost the house. But when I had a court order they [the local authority] told me they wouldn't help until the bailiffs changed the locks.

Obviously you worry about where you are going and whether you'll be on the streets. When you've got a child the idea of living in a hostel is worrying too.

Very few of those who had their home repossessed ended up on the streets, but many had to move into temporary and unsuitable accommodation.

The B and B was just temporary and then the council found us a permanent place. It was hell – it was terrible – you just couldn't sleep at night as it was near a pub/club. People knocked on the door and the children couldn't go out to play.

My mother's place was too small and we stayed in a caravan in the garden.

Having been through these experiences, their problems were rarely over. People who had been disconnected from their fuel or water supplies were often confronted by reconnection fees. In the case of water, they also had court costs added to their arrears.

It was a lot of money to round up . . . We really didn't have enough to eat that week, because I'd paid them £75. We lived on toast, really, there wasn't substantial meals for the kids.

Those losing their homes faced a whole array of charges added to their arrears, including interest charges; arrears management charges, their lender's legal costs, court charges and the costs of selling their property. These added substantially to the level of their debt.

In addition, many of them carried the additional burden of negative equity. These people faced the prospect of being pursued for the shortfalls of many thousands of pounds, which it would take them years to repay. One unemployed man, for example, was attempting to repay the £5,000 he owed at the rate of £3 a week.

(Grant, 1995; Ford, 1994; Herbert and Kempson, 1995.)

Poor health

The links between income and health are also well established and health differentials have widened in the past ten years. It seems, however, that it is inequality of income, rather than absolute poverty levels, that has contributed to inequality of health, although the reasons for this are by no means clear (Dowler and Calvert, 1995). Poor diet, inadequate housing (including homelessness), job insecurity and financial worries all seem to play a part.

Links with diet

As we have seen, people living on low incomes tend to have diets that are low in fresh fruits and high in fat content. Moreover, the research showed there was a strong association between poverty and unhealthily low intakes of key nutrients (iron, vitamin C, fibre and folate), especially for parents.

Iron	Increases resistance to infection, anaemia and general debilitation
Vitamin C	Maintains healthy skin, teeth, gums and blood vessels; increases the absorption of iron from non-meat sources; and may protect against coronary heart disease and certain cancers.
Fibre	Reduces the risk of constipation, irritable bowel syndrome and colonic cancer.
Folate	Essential for growth and body maintenance. Diets low in folate can lead to anaemia and poor growth in children.

The effects of a poor diet were obvious in many households – with the women bearing the brunt. Cynthia, for example, had sacrificed her diet for her children and suffered from depression as a result of money worries.

> *I don't bother with food. You get pissed off with it. You feel that rotten, really tired and weak. They won't even give you vitamin tablets from the doctors.*

The problem was worse still for people who needed special diets for health reasons such as diabetes and heart conditions. Such diets were usually more expensive to maintain and a low income made it impossible to stick to them rigidly. People usually heeded the advice of doctors at first, but soon found that it was more than they could afford.

> *I'm on what you call a highline diet, with me diabetes. But some weeks it goes out of the window. You can't afford to buy a special diet for me . . . It is a very expensive diet. Sometimes I've had to really cut down with food . . . As a diabetic I shouldn't – I can't go without food. But the things I should really eat, I can't.*

> *A while ago he [her husband] was told he had to watch his blood pressure and he was given a diet sheet telling him what he could and couldn't eat. We tried it for a while but the rest of the family didn't like it, so I was having to cook stuff for him and then more for the rest of us. And the low fat things are more expensive . . . I know that if the doctor says you're to do this, then we should do it, but we couldn't manage it. Maybe it was just will power and we should have tried harder, but there is only so much you can do. It's not like we have the money to buy lots of different foods, if I buy something different then I have to not buy something else.*

(Dobson *et al*, 1994; Dowler and Calvert, 1995; Grant, 1995; Kempson *et al*, 1994; Middleton *et al*, 1994; Speak *et al*, 1995.)

Importance of heating

Warmth and lack of dampness are essential for people with arthritic, circulatory or respiratory diseases. Yet there were many examples of people with these conditions who could not afford to heat their homes. Alice, a pensioner, was one of these. She had very bad arthritis and, as she could not afford to heat her home, she spent quite a bit of time in bed.

> *In bed it's freezing and if you saw the things I wear in bed to keep warm it's unbelievable. But I hurt when I'm not very warm, it's the arthritis. It really hurts when it's too blooming cold.*

Sunil's wife had a circulatory disorder and she had been told to keep warm and bathe in warm water. But lack of money meant that they sat cloaked in blankets while their children were at school during the day.

> *She's [referring to his wife] got a tickling finger, she went to the hospital for using cold water instead of hot water . . . the doctors advised always to keep warm, use hot water, stay in the warm. When we think of the bill coming through . . .*

(Grant, 1995; Herbert and Kempson, 1995; Kempson *et al*, 1994; Morris and Ritchie, 1994; Speak *et al*, 1995.)

Effects of poor housing and homelessness

There is a well-established relationship between inadequate housing and poor health, which is illustrated by the qualitative research. In one family, the mother and both children suffered from asthma, which was aggravated by the damp housing they had been allocated since having their home repossessed. In another, a child had severe asthma attacks as a result of the mould growing on the walls of their flat. Constant condensation caused a permanent damp problem, which persisted even though the council stripped off the plaster twice a year. But any hopes of rehousing seemed remote as they had rent arrears.

But the most extreme cases of ill-health were to be found among those who were homeless, although the links between health and homelessness were hard to disentangle. Health problems made it more difficult for people to find and keep accommodation and many people felt that their health had deteriorated as a result of being homeless.

> *It certainly affects your health . . . your body gets completely run down . . . you're not eating properly, you're not sleeping properly and you're not getting proper heat.*

Single homeless people reported more health problems than the general population and those sleeping rough were at even greater risk. They were especially prone to problems that were linked to lack of shelter or warmth: chronic chest or breathing problems, wounds, skin ulcers and other skin conditions, and musculoskeletal problems.

My asthma's been getting worse since I was homeless, my asthma's got worse and worse . . . when I was on the street it was very bad.

If you're homeless and on the street, you can pick up all sorts of diseases. You get scabies, all sorts, skin diseases, that's a common one.

Mental health problems were also more prevalent among single homeless people compared with the general population. In many cases being homeless had aggravated an existing problem.

I get depressed and that's why, sometimes, I can have this mad kind of fit. I can sit there and talk to myself and I will just go in some weird freaky way.

While in others, homelessness had precipitated the illness. One woman, for example, described how homelessness had triggered a whole series of events which finally led to depression.

When I first got evicted, I think everything seemed to go wrong. I couldn't get to college, I had no money, couldn't get my housing benefit, the problems just kept piling up and up, so I got a bit depressed.

(Bines, 1994; Ford, 1994; Grant, 1995; Kempson *et al*, 1994; Speak *et al*, 1995.)

Money worries
Losing a job and continual worries about money can take a toll on the health of people even when they have a home to live in. The stress, depression and despair associated with living on a low income is best described in the words of those who have experienced them.

What has happened to me now is that I'm so fed up of the whole situation; I think I've lost interest. It's like it's day in, day out, it's the same thing. There is no let up and you get tired of trying to figure up, well what to cook, well how will I make this money do the job of three or four times the amount and then you can't do it. I mean that doesn't stop the bills coming in . . . then the debt collectors come . . . people think you're getting this big set of money . . . If you could get a job that pays you a decent wage . . . It's this modern life of not being able to pay your way, to live an ordinary life – go out and buy basics without having to count up in the supermarket. Every time you buy something you count it up in your head just to make sure, when you get to the checkout, you've got enough . . . People like me – we do this every single day of our lives, the strain must tell somehow. (Divorced woman, in her fifties, claiming Income Support and living with her dependent daughter and independent son)

Not being able to sleep, that's what gets me. I'm alright during the day, with two of them – too busy to think about it much. At night when they're in bed, you start thinking, how am I going to pay this or that. Then by the time I go to bed I can't sleep – takes me hours sometimes. He [the doctor] gave me some tablets but I daren't take them, couldn't wake up next morning, and I'm scared if I don't hear the bairns in the night. Anyway I don't need tablets, I need £200. (Young single mother with two children, living on Income Support)

I have quite bad depression. I take anti-depressants every day. And I know that depression is a contributory factor in rheumatoid arthritis. But, nevertheless, it is the financial situation ... I still hanker after the days, which I know aren't going to come back unless we win the pools or something like that. I think it's hard to cope with. But you don't have any option. You just have to get on with it. (Married man who was disabled and out of work)

Faced with mounting debts and no obvious way out of their financial difficulties, a number of people had seriously contemplated suicide. Mr and Mrs Brown were both in their mid-fifties and disabled. Mrs Brown had a spinal injury from an industrial accident, while Mr Brown had had two heart attacks and was diabetic. They realised that neither of them would work again and, as they struggled to live on benefits, were falling into arrears with their mortgage, a secured loan and other bills. This took a toll on both of them.

We felt, you know, as if we were in the gutter. I've been in a right state. I've seen my wife sat in this chair here with a piece of paper and pen working it out – who can we pay what, week in, week out. And that must have been a tremendous strain on her and she battled through. I'm sorry I can't do that. I'd much rather, when it comes to a real push, go out there and jump under a bus. You might think I'm just saying this, but I'm telling you, when it gets to that stage I've gone to bed and I've said – 'I wish to God he'd let me go'. I've laid in bed night after night, unbeknownst to her, and I've prayed to God 'Please let me go, please let me have another [heart attack], let's get out of this'.

Jim had a history of mental illness, which deteriorated when he got into debt.

> *I was missing this and trying to avoid that and, in the end, I just didn't know where to turn. And things seemed to get from bad to worse from there. My mental health deteriorated as well and the more debt I got into the more my mental health deteriorated . . . until I was admitted to hospital as a suicide risk.*

While Carol's brother-in-law had actually committed suicide because of debt problems.

> *He had all these debts. He couldn't cope with it. He committed suicide. That's what it does to people. When they lose their job they get so much in debt, people do that. They can't cope with it.*

(Grant, 1995; Herbert and Kempson, 1995; Kempson *et al*, 1994; Morris and Ritchie, 1994; Speak *et al*, 1995.)

Summary

A low income affects people's lives in many ways. It generally means having no social life, with families spending a lot of time at home together. This can cement relationships but more often it places a strain on them, resulting in family breakdown in extreme cases.

It leads to poor diets, with people often having to choose between eating healthy foods or having sufficient to eat, and to economies in the use of heating and water. These, in turn, contribute to health problems as does inadequate housing.

Money worries are common in low-income households and debts mainly occur through lack of money rather than fecklessness or attempts to avoid payment. Unsympathetic creditors can add to the anxieties people face, so that debt, too, takes a toll on people's physical and mental health.

3 Varying experiences of poverty

The previous two chapters have taken an overview of life on a low income, but people's experiences of poverty differ quite markedly one from another. Income levels inevitably play a big part, but so too does the length of time people have lived on a low income and their approaches to making ends meet. At the same time it is clear that there are circumstances – most of them beyond the control of the individuals concerned – that act to make a difficult situation either better or worse. Family circumstances, support networks and family relationships, where people live, health and even the time of year all play an important part in the subjective experience of poverty.

Income levels

It is hardly surprising that income levels make a difference to people's experience of poverty. But more remarkable is just how little extra money it takes to make a significant impact on people's lives.

Without a doubt, those living on Income Support faced the greatest struggle in making ends meet – especially if they had deductions from their benefit for arrears or a Social Fund loan.

In contrast, families that had incomes just above the Income Support rates (including those who were eligible for Family Credit) found it easier to manage than people who relied solely on benefits. Although they also had little room for manoeuvre, they generally avoided the crises that were so common among Income Support claimants. They were less likely to be constantly in debt, they succeeded more often in ring-fencing money for food and bills, and they did not need to rely so heavily on family and friends for help. A little more money again meant that people had a better quality of life. They ate better, were able to have the occasional 'treat' and did not have to watch the money quite as carefully.

Small sums of additional money were often sufficient to help those in serious financial difficulties to begin to get their situation under control. In one case, the £15 that a lone mother on Income Support earned feeding cats helped her to arrest the slide into arrears and begin paying back some of the money she owed.

I haven't paid them all off, just the most urgent ones . . . this job of feeding cats will probably save me. Basically, if I hadn't found this job I don't know what I would have done.

When asked how much extra money would enable them to make ends meet, lone mothers living on Income Support most commonly put the sum at just £10 a week. The more objective measures described above (comparing the situations of people on Family Credit and Income Support) would put the figure nearer to £20 or even £30 a week.

(Dobson *et al*, 1994; Kempson *et al*, 1994; Morris and Ritchie, 1994; Speak *et al*, 1995.)

Length of time on a low income

People's experiences change the longer they live on a low income – from acute worry initially, through a period when they feel they are coping with the situation, and finally to chronic despair when they can see no light at the end of the tunnel.

Money management was most difficult for people who had just started claiming benefit and, as a consequence, this was a time when they ran a very high risk of getting into arrears. Commitments taken on at a time when their income was sufficient to meet them frequently became unmanageable when they lived on benefit.

The reason we have been in financial difficulty is purely and simply because of the amount of money I earned. We could afford to do these things and then suddenly, within a month, everything changes and you've no longer got that money and its 'Oh God, what do we do now?'

People with savings and assets drew heavily on them to keep afloat, especially if they were looking for another job. But, if they remained on a low income for any length of time, they soon found their savings had been eroded. For example, Paul and Sue had both been in well-paid jobs in the past and had standing orders to pay £200 a month into their savings and had £10,200 put by. But Sue had gone from full-time to part-time working and shortly afterwards Paul lost his job. He eventually found another job, but only part-time as an insurance agent. They drew on their savings to keep up with their bills and mortgage and also to buy a car for Paul to use in his new job.

We were doing quite well at one stage – I think we had quite a bit of savings when we last spoke to you. But then we re-carpeted the house and done other things and bought a car ... Having just paid £500 mending the car we've got about £480. That's it, that's going to be it, because we can't afford to save now.

People who had little or no savings when their incomes dropped found it difficult to adjust their lifestyle, and often their entire income was less than they had previously spent on food alone. The risk of debt in these circumstances was very high.

The longer they lived on low incomes the better some people seemed to cope, indeed managing a very low-income budget became a way of life. Many reflected on how they seemed to make ends meet more frequently than had been the case in the past.

I don't have any more money than I used to when I first started on benefit, it's just that now I know what I can and can't do. I'm always looking ahead and so long as things don't catch me unawares then we're alright. It's hard always without money – you don't stop. But we manage and that's something.

We cope with money and that but you can't forget about it; you're always thinking I need money for this and money for that. It's all the time.

But in the long-term, life on a low income began to get people down. Most of those who had been poor for a number of years spoke of how depressed they felt. Marion and her friend, Jenny, summed up how many others in the same position felt.

Marion: There's not enough money to pay what you've got to pay – it seems like I'm in a poverty trap. I really, really try, but I just can't financially get myself clear. Every year it seems to get worse.

Jenny: She sat down and sobbed the other day about debts, asking me what she was going to do.

As clothing and footwear wore out and household goods and equipment needed to be repaired or replaced, there were obvious signs of strain on household budgets. Lack of savings often meant using credit, placing a further drain on resources. Moreover, studies of nutrition have found that the longer people lived on benefit the worse were their diets – partly because of these drains on their incomes and partly because shopping and cooking became a chore.

(Dobson *et al*, 1994; Dowler and Calvert, 1995; Grant, 1995; Herbert and Kempson, 1995; Kempson *et al*, 1994; Morris and Ritchie, 1994; Speak *et al*, 1995.)

Approaches to making ends meet

Although income levels have a very significant influence on the quality of people's lives, they are far from the whole story. Approaches to money management also play an important role.

Budgeting styles were most likely to make a difference to the quality of life for people with incomes that were above Income Support levels. Those who planned their budget were less likely either to have to go without essentials like food and fuel at the end of the week or to fall behind with their bills.

But among the very poorest families, careful money management alone was unlikely to improve their quality of life. Those living on benefits generally faced a difficult choice between cutting back drastically on essentials or falling behind with their bills. These two approaches led to rather different experiences of poverty.

Those who cut back constantly worried about money. They often went without food entirely for short periods and lived in unheated homes, both of which took a toll on their physical health. Their lives tended to be little more than a basic existence.

> *I don't smoke, I don't drink, I don't go out, I don't eat meat. I have thought of getting rid of the TV, but I can't because it's for [my son] . . . I think 'Shall I get rid of the cat?' But I can't . . . There's absolutely nothing I spend my money on except just surviving, you know, paying bills and buying food. That's all I spend my money on.*

Some suffered extreme social isolation to avoid spending money, such as Maria, a young divorced mother who normally only went out once a week – to buy food at the local market. She said that when money was very tight 'I can't go out at all: I have to stay at home'. Her husband gave her no maintenance and she literally had to beg him to help her pay large bills. Normally he waited until she was reduced to tears before giving into her requests. Maria worried that her five-year-old son saw her as a drudge, while his father would take him out for the weekend and shower him with treats.

A small number of women had remained in violent relationships rather than get into debt. Domestic violence and withholding money seemed often to go hand-in-hand. Sally had left her husband after a particularly bad beating. She did not qualify for Income Support as he was supposed to pay her maintenance, which she never received. Mounting money problems, which were affecting her young daughters, persuaded her to return to her husband.

In contrast, people who delayed paying their bills, rather than cut back on food and heating, paid dearly for it in the longer term. It was not long before they got into serious arrears and faced the worries of having creditors chasing them.

> *You just wish you could win the pools. For us to get up in the morning and have peace of mind. It hits you debt – as soon as you wake up. To wake up knowing there's nothing there . . . It's something nobody should have to endure.*

> *I panic every time when I get warning letters from everyone. I panic 'Oh they're going to break in, they're going to get keys to get into my place and when I go home I'm going to find everything gone'.*

Whereas the careful money managers cut back on heating and (if it was metered) on their use of water, those who delayed paying bills ran the risk of being cut off. They also lived with the fear of losing their homes. At the extreme, the strain of constantly being in serious debt took a heavy toll to the point where (as seen in Chapter 2) some even considered suicide or turning to crime.

It is impossible to say which approach to making ends meet was the better one. Neither of them enabled people to cope with the problem of living on very low incomes. They simply resulted in different experiences.

(Dobson *et al*, 1994; Grant, 1995; Herbert and Kempson, 1995; Kempson *et al*, 1994; Morris and Ritchie, 1994; Speak *et al*, 1995.)

Family circumstances

Young people who live on low incomes generally find it more difficult to manage than those past retirement age. But their difficulties cannot be attributed entirely to lack of experience of money management – they also face additional expenditure.

Costs of setting up home

Having to furnish and equip homes placed additional strains on low-income budgets. This was a particular problem for young single mothers, who often needed to move into their homes quickly once a tenancy had been accepted and had only rarely acquired much in the way of furniture or equipment. Similar problems existed for young couples when they first married, but they often received smaller household items as presents.

Table 1 Costs of furnishing and household appliances

	New £	Second-hand £	Catalogue £
	£	£	£
Sofa/chair	199	45	480
Table and chairs	60	45	200
Double bed	99	60	150
Single bed	79	25	85
Cooker	239	130	280
Fridge	139	80	190
Washing machine	269	140	280
TV	175	70	240
Carpet 16 sq yds	48	N/A	60
Total cost	£1,307	£595	£1,965

Note: Prices from Newcastle shops and catalogues, 1994.

Source: Speak *et al*, 1995.

A study of single mothers in Newcastle has provided details of the basic costs of furnishing and equipping a home. This showed that young people faced costs of between £700 and £1,500, depending on whether they bought second-hand goods or new. Finding these sums of money was very difficult for those living on benefits or wages of £100 a week or less. And second-hand goods were often found to be a false economy. The trend among the middle classes of buying old (especially stripped pine) furniture has pushed up prices of all but the cheap mass-produced items in poor condition. The life expectancy of these goods was not long.

Faced with these problems many people had decided buy on credit, using mail-order catalogues, where they could spread the costs over periods of up to 100 weeks. But bargains were hard to come by and the costs of buying all their furnishings and household appliances this way would have been £2,000, incurring over £30 a week in repayments. These extra demands on their income made it all the more likely that they would get into financial difficulties.

(Kempson *et al*, 1994; Speak *et al*, 1995.)

Table 2 Total cost of basic household equipment

16-piece crockery set
16-piece cutlery set
Kitchen utensils
3 saucepans
Oven dishes/bowls

Duvet and cover
1 pillow and pillow case
4 hand towels
2 bath towels

Bucket and mop
Sweeping brush
Hand brush and dustpan
Iron and ironing board
Washing line and pegs

Total cost Basic quality £102; Standard quality £166

Note: Prices from Woolworths and Poundstretcher, 1994.

Source: Source: Speak *et al*, 1995.

The costs of children

Children, too, placed a strain on household budgets. Childbirth was often accompanied by a drop in income if the mother gave up work. It was also a time when people faced high capital costs as well as an increase in their outgoings on food and clothes.

While parents were prepared to make do or buy second-hand for themselves, they almost invariably wanted to give their children the best. This was especially true for newborn babies. Yet, according to the study in Newcastle, equipping and clothing a baby cost at least £500 – considerably more than the £100 maternity grant received by mothers living on Income Support.

Baby clothes and equipment may, to some extent, be provided by friends and family – either as new gifts for the baby or as hand-ons from older children. But not every mother received help in this way. Consequently there were mothers who relied on mail-order catalogues for many of their baby things. The weekly repayments of buying the basic lists of equipment and clothing through a catalogue would be around £18.

Table 3 Costs of basic baby equipment

	Basic quality £	Standard quality £	Catalogue £
Cot	80	164	100
Carry cot/pushchair	189	268	245
Standard buggy	40	119	30
High chair	40	60	30
Cot linen	64	80	66
Bottles and steriliser	14	17	35
Stair gate	22	25	35
Total cost	449	733	541

Note: Prices from Mothercare and mail-order catalogues, 1994.

Source: Speak *et al*, 1995.

Table 4 Total cost of basic baby clothes for newborn baby

6 vests
6 baby grows
4 plastic pants
4 cardigans
2 bonnets
1 shawl
2 pairs mittens

Total price £59

Note: Prices were taken from typical market shops in Newcastle, 1994.

Source: Speak *et al*, 1995.

In another study, groups of parents from different socio-economic backgrounds and living in different parts of the country were asked to draw up 'minimum essential' requirements for children of different ages. These were subsequently costed by researchers using 'middle-of-the-range' stores.

When shown the costings, even the parents on Income Support felt that they could not cut back any further. Regardless of income, they agreed that it was the basic minimum that needed to be spent on a child and felt that, in reality, they would have wanted to spend more.

> *Ann: I mean you've not given them the things you'd like to give them, you're only giving them the bare essentials.*

> *Sandy: How would you feel if your children had to manage on that?*

> *Laura: Gutted.*

Yet, depending on the age of their child, their budgets were between £3 and £10 a week more than the Income Support rates for children. The discrepancies were greatest for children aged between two and ten years.

Table 5 Parents' minimum essential budget standard (£ per week)

		Under 2	2–5 years	6–10 years	11–16 years
Food		6.85	9.36	9.72	10.11
Clothes	girl	5.57	7.13	6.94	5.83
	boy	5.41	8.65	6.94	6.34
Possessions and equipment		4.75*	3.13*	2.20	4.13
Activities		1.75	7.53	7.45	7.36
Furniture and decorating		0.17	0.54	0.54	0.54
Laundry		0.86	0.86	0.62	0.62
Toiletries	girl	6.54**	2.18**	0.65	2.45
	boy	6.54**	2.18**	0.65	1.99
Total	*girl*	*26.49*	*30.73*	*28.12*	*31.04*
	boy	*26.33*	*32.25*	*27.67*	*31.09*
IS plus family premium		*20.68*	*20.68*	*20.68*	*28.03*

Notes: 1994 prices at 'middle-of-the-range' stores.
* Includes baby equipment such as pushchair and car seat. ** Includes disposable nappies.

Source: Middleton *et al*, 1994.

Parents also reported frequent requests from schools for financial contributions. School trips, money for items made in craft and technology classes, GCSEs and school uniforms were all areas where parents struggled to find the money required.

Yet, parents in a wide range of research studies were adamant that they would not compromise on spending on their children. They did not want them to be different from other children and to have to bear the stigma of poverty.

Lesley: Which one of us would stand up and make our child stand out?

Chris: That's right you wouldn't.

Diane: Oh no, you'd never want your child to be the one who comes home crying at the end of the day.

Instead, parents bore the brunt of living on a low income. They went without food and did not heat their homes when their children were at school. They borrowed money, bought goods on credit and even delayed bill-paying if their children needed something they could not afford. Families with children therefore had higher levels of arrears than other households, with all the worries and consequences that entailed.

(Dobson *et al*, 1994; Grant, 1995; Kempson *et al*, 1994; Middleton *et al*, 1994; Speak *et al*, 1995.)

Having someone to share the problems with

Managing a low-income budget was stressful to the point that, as we have seen, many couples argued about money and even split up. Those who coped best with living in poverty tended to be couples who had very strong relationships to start with. The old adage that 'a problem shared is a problem halved' seemed to hold true. Indeed, their problems seemed to bring them even closer together.

I think we're just floating now. It's always been a bit tight hasn't it? We've been through worse than this and we've managed. You've got to manage . . . not let it get you down . . . there's always a way.

We are very content, you know, we take each day as it comes . . . we've learnt that you can't always plan ahead . . . things don't always work out as you want ... so you do the best you can. The important thing is to be happy.

Yet both of these couples were living on benefit and had been through very difficult times indeed. The husband of the first couple had been through three redundancies. The first time he had found another job straightaway, the second time he was out of work for three years and, on the most recent occasion he had been unemployed for a year. The second couple had four children and the husband had lost his job 15 years previously because he was epileptic. He had recently had surgery for a brain tumour and was receiving radiation and chemotherapy.

In contrast, adults who lived alone often spoke of the loneliness of living on a low income – in part caused by their inability to afford a social life, but also derived from the stigma they felt being poor. In these circumstances loss of self-esteem and confidence was commonplace.

Many disabled people lived isolated lives, especially if their impairment limited their mobility and they lived alone. Those who faced debt problems alone experienced this loneliness very deeply.

You feel degraded. You think other people know that you are in debt. You think you've done something wrong . . . it's very lonely because you don't tell anyone. I never tell [my sons] things like that, no. I don't mention it to them. I think it's like I'm saying to myself I can manage.

Young single mothers also experienced loneliness at home with their new babies. Although there were mother and toddler groups in the inner cities, very young mothers felt excluded because of their age.

I don't go. They look at you like you're a slag . . . 'cos I was so young like . . . 15 when I had her. It's for older mothers, they're all older you know, 20 and that.

In rural areas the stigma of being a single mother was very strong.

There's not a lot of young mums around here, not as young as me anyway, and they mostly have blokes. People look at you funny. I can't go anywhere to meet other mums 'cos there isn't any. It's just me and the baby all day.

(Dobson *et al*, 1994; Grant 1995; Kempson *et al*, 1994; Middleton *et al*, 1994; Speak *et al*, 1995.)

Health and disability

We have already seen that people's health is affected by living in poverty – through poor diet, poor housing, unemployment and worries about financial problems. At the same time, sickness and disability are the reason why some people live on low incomes – either because they cannot work or because they have given up work to care for others.

At the same time, living on a low income was found to be more difficult for people who were sick or disabled, or their carers, than it was for those in good health. In part this was because financial worries compounded the other difficulties they had. For example, Wendy's husband had walked out shortly after their now two-year-old daughter was born with cerebral palsy. This left her to look after her daughter and two other children on a low income.

> I mean every time these letters [from the building society] came through they just caused me more distress. I mean, I have got enough on my plate with her without all this extra worrying whether I was going to keep a roof over my head.

In addition, many sick and disabled people had additional expenses to meet from their incomes. These included special diets; extra heating; extra hot water; higher telephone bills; high transport costs; frequent replacement of clothing and bedding; the costs of care and support services; and prescription charges. The benefits system acknowledges that disabled people face additional costs. Some of those claiming Income Support are eligible for a premium payment on top of basic rates, and the recently introduced Disability Living Allowance (DLA) is designed to assist specific groups of disabled people. However, additional expenses were frequently not covered by the basic Income Support premium and many disabled people either failed to apply for or failed to qualify for DLA (see Chapter 7).

(Grant, 1995; Kempson et al, 1994.)

Family and support networks

Most people who lived on low incomes received financial help and support from friends and family. And the poorer they were, the more they relied on them for necessities. There was also a great deal of reciprocity, with people helping one another out as and when they could. As a consequence the people who experienced the worst aspects of living on a low income were often those who, for one reason or another, had no-one they could turn to for help.

Help with 'luxuries'

Help from relatives who were better off allowed some people to take holidays, to have days or evenings out and to have the occasional 'treat'.

They will take [my wife] out to bingo . . . to give her a break because we can't afford it . . . and come in with fresh meat . . . my parents will come down and take us out for the day.

The only time we travel is when we go to Scotland, 'cos my auntie's got a farmhouse there, so we stay there for free. But I have to find the transport. Mum gives me half, which was £20. I didn't have to pay for my daughter last time because she was under five.

Grandparents, in particular, often paid for school trips, gave children 'treats' and bought them the presents they craved for Christmas or their birthday.

My dad always says, 'These [his grandchildren] are not going to go short. You want it, you've got it. Don't ever say you've got nothing for these.' . . . They're both pensioners. They've got a bit of money because my dad was injured in the war and they've backdated his war pension. Without my parents, I don't think I would manage as well as what we do.

(Kempson *et al*, 1994; Middleton *et al*, 1994; Morris and Ritchie 1994; Speak *et al*, 1995.)

Help with furniture and household equipment

Young people often received help when they set up home, although the extent of that help depended on how well off their friends and family were. Some were bought new things, others had to make do with things that were passed on second-hand. Either way, it avoided their having to use credit.

When household appliances broke down, friends and relatives also helped to replace them where they could. Help with redecorating homes or repairing household appliances was more common still.

(Jones, 1995; Kempson *et al*, 1994; Morris and Ritchie, 1994; Speak *et al*, 1995.)

Help with making ends meet

The most common type of help, however, was assistance in making ends meet. But people clearly found some types of help more acceptable than others. Help in kind was considered better than cash, and loans were better than gifts – especially gifts of cash, which were seen as charity and to be avoided wherever possible. Being able to reciprocate in some way was essential to maintaining dignity.

Clothing was a common, and also the most acceptable, form of help. Passing on clothes that were not worn out was seen as a sensible use of resources and parents welcomed gifts of new clothing for their children at Christmas or their birthdays.

Help with food, too, was fairly common. This included being asked to stay for a meal, receiving gifts of home-grown vegetables and, most commonly, borrowing food when they ran short.

> I've got my mum down the road, so she's quite handy. Mostly I run out of teabags and such. I've never really run out of food because I've got too many friends around. I can always go to them.

Even so, by far the most common form of help was small loans, enabling people to survive until the next pay or benefit day. In many communities there was a constant round of lending and borrowing small sums – usually less than £5 – for a few days.

> My mum and dad, they help us out. Like yesterday, I had run out of nappies, we had no bread, no eggs and we hadn't even got a tin of beans in the cupboard. And I rang up my mum . . . my dad lent me £5. So I managed to get a loaf of bread, ten nappies and some potatoes and my mum lent me a tin of beans and a tin of rice pudding.

Mothers and daughters and female friends regularly helped one another out in this way and could not have managed without it.

Families also helped out when people fell into debt – paying off the arrears when they could afford to do so or lending the money needed when they could not.

(Dobson et al, 1994; Grant, 1995; Herbert and Kempson, 1995; Herbert and Kempson, 1996; Kempson et al, 1994; Morris and Ritchie, 1994; Speak et al, 1995.)

Limitations on help

Although it was common to receive help from friends and family, there were limitations. In many cases whole families were in the same boat and, while they helped with small sums to make ends meet, they could not afford to do more even if they wanted to.

> *I've still got my dear little mum, who is an OAP and she sends me £10, once in a blue moon, but she can't afford to and it's so sweet of her, it makes me cry when she does that . . . It's like families looking after their own isn't it?*

> *There's been weeks when there just hasn't been the money, and I worry about what we'll do. I mean there's no money even if I don't pay the bills one week, what can I do except ask me mam? I know she'll help but she hasn't got much either, so it's a question of borrowing food and that, toilet rolls, things like that. I don't often borrow money off her unless I'm really desperate, I suppose because she hasn't got it and because I would have to pay it back.*

In other cases people disliked asking for help and only did so with reluctance. This was especially the case where friends and family were better off and people wanted to retain their self-reliance and independence. They thought such help was charity and to be avoided at all costs.

> *Even when I had nothing, I wouldn't go to my family. I wouldn't degrade myself.*

> *I hate it. I hate asking for it and it's given very, it's not given wholeheartedly. It's, 'Oh, she's got herself in a mess again!' That kind of attitude.*

Young people who had left home early, only to find they could not cope, were also reluctant to turn to parents for help. They felt this was admitting defeat.

> *I've got so much pride about asking people for money. I wouldnae ask them, like my dad or my grandparents. But I knew I could have got it, but I wouldnae ask for it.*

There were also people who, for one reason or another, had no family they could turn to. Parents with young children and young people setting up home had a particularly hard time if they had no-one to turn to for help. For example, Rita, who was a lone mother, had been badly hit when her mother had died the previous year. She had previously kept up with her bills but, since her mother's death, she had fallen into arrears.

I'm worse now 'cos my mum's died. She used to help me out so I'm worse even . . . She used to help me out when I was broke . . . she'd give me a tenner a week or get me some groceries or whatever. But now I just have to make do.

Young people leaving home also had a very hard time if they received no support from their families, often having spells of homelessness. Those at greatest risk were young people who were stepchildren, or who had left homes because of family arguments or, worse still, violence.

(Dobson *et al*, 1994; Grant, 1995; Herbert and Kempson, 1996; Jones, 1995; Kempson *et al*, 1994; Morris and Ritchie, 1994; Speak *et al*, 1995.)

Locality and neighbourhood

Experiences of poverty differ from one part of the country to another. There are two main reasons for this. There are geographical variations in the costs of basic household services which mean that people with similar incomes have different levels of outgoings depending on where they live. But there are also significant differences between the neighbourhoods people live in. Being poor in a rural village is a different experience from poverty on an inner city housing estate.

Variations in the cost of living

Housing costs, local taxes, water charges and fuel bills all vary from one part of the country to another – to an extent that can be quite significant for people living on low incomes.

There are wide variations in the rents charged by local authorities, but Housing Benefit removes the immediate impact of these. The same is not true for home owners who, if they work, receive no assistance at all with their housing costs. Yet house prices vary a great deal regionally.

There are wide variations in the levels of Council Tax set by local authorities. Councils also vary in the charges made for home-care services to elderly and disabled people. Some do not charge people on Income Support at all, while others expect them to make a contribution towards the costs.

Water charges vary significantly between water companies – by as much as £3 a week. For people living on Income Support this is a significant sum of money and it is not surprising that those with the very highest water bills (of more than £5 a week) had a very high risk of getting into arrears, especially if they lived on low incomes and had young children.

Although charges for fuel do not vary regionally, the need for heating does. As a consequence people living in colder parts of the country more often face the dilemma of going without heating or finding the extra money to keep warm.

(Grant, 1995; Herbert and Kempson, 1995.)

Inner city housing estates and rural villages

The neighbourhoods that people live in make quite a difference to their experiences of living on a low income. These can be brought into sharpest focus by looking at the two extremes: inner city housing estates and rural villages.

With the sale of over one million council houses, many of the properties that remain in urban areas are on inner city housing estates. Homes that were offered to single mothers, people whose homes had been repossessed and others needing to rent for the first time were often on 'hard-to-let' estates. But while the individual flats themselves were in a bad condition, it was more often the neighbourhood as a whole that got people down. Crime and vandalism were a particular concern, especially to parents of children.

> *This area is not a good one to raise children. Kids start fires and race cars up and down – it's a rough estate.*

> *The police are constantly being called out because of fights, drinking and drugs.*

> *You see them . . . all at the back of the garages at night. They're sniffing like . . . and other stuff. They don't even hide it, you can see the bags and things in the morning. The bairns pick stuff up. I've reported it but they didn't do nowt.*

> *My daughter was sexually threatened by a young boy and his family have threatened me.*

Fears about crime and violence on inner city estates meant that children were not allowed to play out of doors and some parents hardly dared go out themselves. They also led to sleepless nights.

> *I can't sleep, me. Just keep thinking, every little noise, they're going to break in. Aint got nowt, like. Don't know what they'd want to get in here for, but I still can't sleep for it. It makes you sick after a while . . . worrying and no sleep and the bairns and that.*

Pensioners and people nearing retirement also spoke of their fears and experiences living on inner city estates.

I don't go out any more. I only go to the paper shop and come back, about as far as I dare go . . . It frightens me this area . . . I just walk in here and bolt and chain that door every time and lock it.

I've been broke into twice. First time they pinched me pension books, mobility books; the next time they broke in they pinched my remote control television . . . my wireless and me watch . . . I was out one day, 20 minutes, went to the shop down there. When I come back, no windows, they broke the lot . . . Smoking drugs next door, shouting and bawling, four o'clock in the morning taxis come up, shouting and bawling . . .

By stark contrast, people living on low incomes in rural Scotland felt they had a much better quality of life, which was often expressed in terms of the *lack* of crime and vandalism.

We never lock a door here. When you go to bed here, you are peaceful and you know nobody is going to come in and rob you, nobody is going to come and murder you.

Well, I mean, Dundee is only 20 miles from here. They've got rapes, murders, drugs, you name it. You can't believe there's just 20 miles from here and there's none of that here.

It's much better for the kids to be here, although for us there are big drawbacks to living here . . . It's better for our kids because it's so much safer, there's less drugs and less violence than there is in [our home town], which has got a bit wild now.

Although people living in rural areas had greater peace of mind, there *were* drawbacks. Their subjective assessment of their poverty or disadvantage tended to be at odds with objective definitions. There was, for example, an acute lack of affordable housing to rent, so that many young couples started their married lives without a proper home, living in temporary lets or caravans. Jobs were scarce and very low paid when they were available. Local facilities, including shops, were few and far between. And these problems were all compounded by either expensive transport or none at all.

This suggests that people's own ideas about what constitutes poverty are informed by a picture of life on an inner city housing estate. The problems that poor people face living in rural areas are interpreted by them as arising from the fact that they live in remote communities, not from their poverty. Yet none of the problems above would affect people who are more affluent to anything like the same degree.

(Power and Tunstall, 1995; Shucksmith *et al*, 1994; Speak *et al*, 1995.)

Time of the year

Some times of the year are more difficult financially than others – with winter presenting particular problems for people living on low incomes.

During the winter months there were higher fuel bills. Where people had pre-payment meters they felt the effects of this as soon as the weather turned cold. And if their meters were recalibrated to collect arrears, they faced very heavy costs indeed during the winter months.

> *In the winter . . . if I have the heating on it's going to cost me about £5 a day, 'til I've got my arrears paid. I dread the winter coming.*

Those who could afford to tried to top up their meter in advance of the cold weather. That way they could not touch the money they had put aside for fuel. In contrast, people who were billed quarterly faced their greatest problems when they received their winter bills. As a consequence, there was a clear seasonality to fuel debt and disconnection.

Parents also commented on the additional cost of clothing their children in winter.

> *Summer you can kit them out very cheaply with T-shirts and things off the market, a pair of sandals or trainers. Winter comes, and they've got to have jackets and tights. They go to school and get through tights at about two pairs a week . . . They've got to have school shoes, they've got to have trainers, hats, gloves, scarves.*

> *I had to kit her out completely for school for winter: coat, shoes, boots, leggings, the lot! And that was just one child! So that £104 [child benefit for all her children] just paid for the one child to be kitted out for winter . . . That was no going stupid and going to expensive shops. That was literally shopping all day in Leicester looking for the best bargains for the money.*

School holidays brought additional financial strains for parents. During cold weather it meant that they spent more on heating because, as one parent put it, 'although we can sit in our coats, you can't expect the children to'. Children who normally had school meals had to be fed and parents who worked had to pay for childminding. Moreover, when the weather was bad, children could not go out to play and this often placed a further strain on family relationships where parents did not work.

Christmas was a specially difficult time, when people felt the strain and the stigma of being poor. They often tried to tried to put money on one side for food and presents, but if they lived on a very low income the amounts saved were small.

> *I hated Christmas. I would have preferred it for people not to give me anything because I wouldn't have felt obligated to give back. I found it very hard . . . Like in November, if I found I had a pound or two to spare, I would put it into a jar . . . I gave them all some little thing each, but you feel like it is nothing.*

For parents with young children the desire to give them a happy Christmas took precedence over just about everything else. As a consequence Christmas was often the time when they took on credit commitments to buy presents for their children. It was also when they were very likely to fall behind with their bills. As one mother put it:

> *We're going to live off fresh air, all for a Nintendo game.*

(Grant, 1995; Kempson *et al*, 1994; Middleton *et al*, 1994.)

Experience of poverty within the household

Even within households, experiences of poverty can differ. Men often struggle to come to terms with failing to succeed as the breadwinner, while women bear the brunt of having to manage inadequate resources. Children are particularly susceptible to the stigma of poverty, so that parents often try to shield them whenever they can.

Men
Men experienced feelings of worthlessness and loss of identity when they were out of work or unable to earn a decent wage. Older men and those who had been in well-paid, white-collar jobs were hit particularly hard.

I feel totally wasted to be honest with you. I can tell you, but I don't tell [my wife] very often, but I get quite depressed sometimes when I think about where we were.

I'm too old at 40. Ready for the heap. It's terrible.

Belief in the male breadwinner was felt remarkably strongly, so that men who could not fulfil that role suffered as a consequence. This was especially so when they had young children.

. . . nothing hurts you more than when your kids ask you for something and you look around all four corners and you can't see any way of getting it. At that particular time you feel just like picking up a knife and slitting your throat . . . Sometimes you wish you didn't have kids . . . and I love them more than anything else in the world.

Men also felt cut off socially when they were out of work. With no money to go out with friends they seldom had any male company – and many of those out of work had been in manual jobs which were an all-male world.

You feel better in yourself if you're working. In work you're not excluded. It's a totally different world.

With a job there's something to look forward to, people to meet.

(Ford *et al*, forthcoming; Kempson *et al*, 1994; Morris and Ritchie, 1994.)

Women

Women were confronted by both the worries and the practicalities of making ends meet. They were the ones who shopped around for cheap food and clothing and who had to juggle the bills. While men saw it as their role to provide, women felt it was their job to spend the little money they had wisely so that their family did not go without. Where there was not enough money to go round, they would therefore go without themselves.

I try to make sure they get [enough food]. But like I cook a meal and, as long as there's plenty for them, I make do with a piece of toast.

The bairn always gets plenty [of food] . . . I see to that like. But I don't think I do. Well I know I don't, not really. That's why I'm tired all the time and ratty, get dead ratty these days . . . can't be bothered with nowt.

*I would go to a jumble sale . . . I can't let my old man know that because he'd go
paranoid . . . but I do go to jumble sales and look for like long shirts and then
leggings and whatever . . . But I can't let him know that, 'cos if he ever found out
I'd been to any places like that I should be shot!*

(Dobson *et al*, 1994; Dowler and Calvert, 1995; Kempson *et al*, 1994; Middleton *et
al*, 1994; Morris and Ritchie, 1994; Speak *et al*, 1995.)

Children

Parents were well aware that, potentially, children stood to suffer the worst
stigma of being poor and sacrifices were made to protect them from the worst
consequences.

*Children can be very mean to each other. I remember being teased at school
because we couldn't afford things and I don't want that to happen to my son.*

Interviews with children confirmed that those who were different in any way
from their peers suffered from teasing at best, to outright bullying at worst.

From an early age they experienced pressures to wear the 'right' clothes, which
on occasions meant wearing the right designer label. When asked what
happened if they were not dressed like their friends, they replied:

You'd feel left out.

*Sometimes, they say 'Look at the horrible clothes that he's got on. I'm not playing
with you, you look horrible.'*

You might get picked on or something like that and you feel really embarrassed.

*They hassle you. They say nasty things like 'You get your shoes from the tip', and
stuff like that.*

They'd get beat up.

Knowing the pressures on their children, low-income parents struggled to buy
not just new clothes but, wherever they could manage it, the right brand of jeans
or trainers.

Food, too, marked out children from low-income families. Free school meals
were a very public stigma which some parents struggled to avoid.

I just don't want any of her friends to know she is on free meals, I just don't.

I'm a bit ashamed to say it, but I don't want other people to know that my child gets free school dinners. When I was at school about 18 years ago you were looked down upon. I had that and I felt ashamed.

Some children who were entitled to free school meals were given packed lunches instead. But the problems did not stop there. If they did not have the 'right' food in their lunch packs their friends would pick on them. One mother could not afford Coca-Cola and bought a supermarket brand instead. But to protect her child from teasing she decanted the cheaper drink into a Coke bottle.

It was also important for children to have the 'right' snack foods to share with others. As one young child put it:

But you have to share . . . Everyone laughs at you, except your best friend.

Besides being made to feel different, children from low-income families experienced other consequences of poverty. Generally they did not have bedrooms of their own and so often played on the streets. Less affluent boys often said they spent their time 'hanging about on the street' , while their better-off peers were more likely to say that they usually played at a friend's home. Although the number involved in crime or drug-taking was small, it was more common among the boys in their early teens who led their lives on the street.

Children who lived in neighbourhoods of high unemployment also tended to have low aspirations for their lives. They were less likely than more affluent children to anticipate getting a job and often set their horizons low.

(Dobson *et al*, 1994; Kempson *et al*, 1994; Middleton *et al*, 1994; Morris and Ritchie, 1994; Speak *et al*, 1995.)

Summary

Several points stand out from this analysis. First and foremost, it is clear how a little extra money can make all the difference between a life that is simply devoid of 'luxuries' and one where there is insufficient money even for essentials like food and heating. People who live on state benefits generally cannot overcome their problems no matter which approach to managing their money they adopt. They merely substitute one set of experiences for another.

While the consequences of living on a low income are wide ranging, actual experiences of poverty differ depending on people's circumstances. It is, however, invidious to say that one group has a worse time than others. There are a number of factors that can compound an already difficult situation. These include: the length of time people have been poor; the approach they take to making ends meet; their family circumstances; ill-health and disability; having no-one to turn to for financial help; the neighbourhood they live in; and even the time of the year. Most of these are beyond the control of the people concerned.

PART TWO

4 Changes in the labour market

Two significant changes in the labour market have contributed to the numbers of people living on low incomes. Overall, there has been an increase in job insecurity. A growth in the number of people losing their jobs, coupled with an increase in the time taken to find another one, have resulted in high levels of unemployment and long-term unemployment in particular. At the same time, there has been a shift from full-time permanent jobs towards more part-time, temporary or casual work, and self-employment. Much of this 'flexible' work is low paid.

Moreover these changes have tended to be concentrated among certain households and, as a consequence, there has been an increasing polarisation between households with two earners and those with none (Joseph Rowntree Foundation, 1995).

The effect of these trends on individuals is illustrated quite graphically by the qualitative research. People claiming Income Support (and therefore with the lowest incomes) typically had broken employment histories dominated by unemployment, chronic job insecurity or very long-term unemployment. When they found work it was casual, part-time and low paid. The couples among them were both usually out of work.

Tom, for example, had been in and out of work for 11 years. When jobs were available he normally worked as a labourer, although he had also tried his hand at taxi driving, but had given that up when he earned only £60 for an 84-hour week. He lost his most recent job when the factory burnt down. When interviewed he was doing occasional casual one-off jobs, most recently having earned £75 cash for clearing the grounds of a local factory.

Mike was 38 and had been a sheet metal worker until he was 26, when he was first made redundant. For the past 12 years he had been in and out of work, mostly doing labouring jobs. His last job had been 'out of town', but had ended during the recent slump in the building trade.

Those claiming in-work benefits had slightly higher incomes and tended also to have more stable work histories. They were either people who had a history of fairly stable but low-paid work, or they had been predominantly in employment but had experienced some job insecurity. Generally they were households with just one low-paid wage earner.

Kazim had been a low-paid factory worker all his working life. He had just changed jobs to a better-paid one as a pleater. Even so his wages were only £100 a week and he received a further £37 a week Family Credit.

Those who had incomes that were at or just below the median male earnings were even more likely to have had stable work histories. They included more people who regularly got overtime and a greater proportion of couples where both partners worked.

Tony was a foundry worker whose basic pay was £156 a week but was supplemented by shift working and overtime. On alternate weeks he worked the day shift with overtime, earning £180, or the night shift, getting £220. Ken, in contrast, was a factory worker earning just £120 a week, with no opportunities for overtime. However, his wife had taken a full-time job as a shop assistant which added a further £77 a week to their income.

(Kempson *et al*, 1994; Morris and Ritchie, 1994.)

High unemployment

Britain has suffered two major recessions over the past 15 years – in the early 1980s and again at the beginning of the 1990s. Over that period, the number of unemployed people has trebled, and has been accompanied by an increase in long-term unemployment of a year or more.

Two main factors have contributed to this long-term rise in unemployment – an increase in the levels of redundancy and job loss and a fall in people's rate of return to work (Gregg and Wadsworth, 1995; Joseph Rowntree Foundation, 1995). And for many people one redundancy is followed by another, often to the point where it is barely distinguishable from long-term unemployment.

I've been made redundant three times. The first time I walked straight into another job. Second time I was out for three years. This time I've been out 12 months. I'm well used to it now.

He's the kiss of death. Wherever he goes he gets made redundant. They close the places.

There are pockets of very high unemployment, especially in the old industrial areas. Yet unemployment is a problem that seriously affects rural areas as well. The decline in agricultural jobs has been every bit as severe and people living in rural Scotland recognised that limited work opportunities were now a fact of rural life. Lack of employment for young people was considered to be the most serious problem that rural communities faced.

(Ford *et al*, forthcoming; Kempson *et al*, 1994; Morris and Ritchie, 1994; Shucksmith *et al*, 1995.)

Commitment to work

There was, however, no lack of commitment to working, even among those who had been unemployed for some time. Getting a job was seen as the best chance people on low incomes had of improving their standard of living or repaying the money owed to creditors.

> *He would love to work. He would do anything that he could get in the building trade, or in shop fitting . . . even if that meant having to be away from us during the week.*

> *I think it's outrageous that a person (again it sounds a bit big-headed) with my skills has to live off the State. I mean I think it's terrible. I think that is an absolute waste of time and taxpayers' money, in my opinion. I would go to work tomorrow.*

> *It's a fact of life, you've got to work. Maybe some people are content with having no spending money, but they haven't got bills, but then they can't get any credit . . . It's the way you're brought up. You know my dad was never unemployed . . . as soon as we left school we went to get a job. The worst thing you could ever do when I lived at home was lose a job.*

Such attitudes are often thought to be confined to older people, yet this last man was only 33.

Some people went to incredible lengths to find work. One man, an unskilled worker who had been unemployed for two years, was so 'ashamed' of being unemployed that he moved home without giving his family a forwarding address. He went to the Jobcentre four times a week, looked for work by going to factory gates and checked the local paper. In total he had sent out 109 letters (which he produced in a folder for the interviewer) in his search for a job.

Many men went out looking for work at factory gates in groups. It was a way of keeping in touch with friends and minimised the feelings of rejection. But as a strategy for finding work it was less than successful.

I look for work with my mates. We go to factories, ask them if they need anyone. But there's nothing around. They're laying blokes off. Everyone feels bad about it.

Indeed, a number of studies have stressed the importance of contacts in finding work. The longer people were out of the labour market, the more they lost their contacts and the harder it was to find work.

They employ now from within, a friend of a friend, a member of the family, that's the ways the [jobs] tend to go. You try to get into [a firm] and, unless you've got a member of the family works there, or a very good record, you ain't going to get in there. It's as simple as that.

For this man, visiting factories on the off chance that there might be work was not an option. He lived on a housing estate some way from possible workplaces and, with Income Support payments of £39 a week after deductions for arrears, he had no money to go looking for work.

I glance through the job sections in the paper because that's about the only contact I've got. Because I've got so much money going out, I can't actively get on a bus and go around industrial estates and go out of the area because I just can't afford to do it. If I was to start taking buses everywhere the only place that money could come from is out of my food money and I'm only left with £16 a fortnight for food and I don't know anyone who can live on that.

For unskilled workers, 'getting on your bike' was not always a realistic option because of the costs involved, coupled with the very low likelihood of finding a job. Unskilled workers in rural areas particularly faced this dilemma. With the rapid decline in jobs, the only hope they had of finding work was to move.

There's just a certain amount of work here and those that are unemployed are unemployed . . . It's all very well saying get on your bike and get a job, but there's just no jobs, and you can't eat scenery.

(Ford *et al*, forthcoming; Kempson *et al*, 1994; Morris and Ritchie, 1994; Shucksmith *et al*, 1995.)

Barriers to working

Few groups of workers have escaped the rise in unemployment, but some have clearly suffered higher levels of joblessness than others. Those who were most likely to have lost their job were also the ones who experienced greatest difficulty finding another one – manual workers, people in their twenties or their fifties, and people in poor health or with disabilities.

Unskilled workers

While the most recent recession triggered increases in redundancies among white-collar workers, unemployment (and especially long-term unemployment) remains a problem which disproportionately affects manual workers (especially those who are unskilled or semi-skilled) and women in routine non-manual jobs (Joseph Rowntree Foundation, 1995).

This was reflected in the research. Men who recounted having the greatest difficulty finding employment were looking for jobs as warehousemen, labourers or unskilled factory workers. The women were looking for cleaning or other unskilled jobs with hours that enabled them to care for their children. Competition for jobs was fierce and when they found work it was usually in an insecure job.

(Ford *et al*, forthcoming; Kempson *et al*, 1994; Morris and Ritchie 1994; Shucksmith *et al*, 1995; Speak *et al*, 1995; Third 1995.)

Age

Age is also a barrier to people finding work and affects both very young people and people in their forties and fifties (Joseph Rowntree Foundation, 1995). The problem facing young people was lack of experience, especially those who left school with few qualifications. To get a job they needed work experience which they could only get by working.

> *You know they were all saying, 'Well, we want two year's experience'. So how are you supposed to get experience if no-one will take you on?*

> *There's no jobs for the young ones – it's just more education or the dole.*

While older people who had been made redundant often found age restrictions on the jobs that were advertised.

> *I'm too old at 40! Ready for the heap. It's terrible, it's just too difficult to get a job at the moment.*

They're taking on the children, well they're taking on young people coming out of college, who've done it on paper, but who've never done it in reality.

(Ford *et al*, forthcoming; Kempson *et al*, 1994; Morris and Ritchie 1994; Shucksmith *et al*, 1995.)

Poor health and disability

Poor health and disability both led to people losing their jobs and made it very difficult for them to find other work. At the time of the research, there was no law that prohibited discrimination against disabled people and many people recounted that they were among the first to lose their jobs when their employer was making workers redundant. In other cases employers were unwilling to offer newly disabled employees alternative employment. One man, a maintenance engineer, had been involved in an accident at work, caused by poor safety procedures.

I went to my doctor and she said 'Well if you carry on doing that job you are going to end up in a wheelchair'. So I went to see a consultant and he kind of confirmed the same thing. He said 'Seek lighter work'. I went back to work, I told the manager and they said 'Well there are no light jobs. The best we can do is offer you voluntary redundancy.'

Having lost their job, people found that other employers were not keen to take on someone who had ill-health or a disability. This was especially the case among older workers who, once they were labelled as having a disability, faced enormous difficulties getting back into work. Despite this, few unemployed disabled people gave up hope of finding a job, even if they were receiving Invalidity Benefit.

(Ford *et al*, forthcoming; Grant 1995; Kempson *et al*, 1994; Shucksmith *et al*, 1995.)

Women returners

Women with children often faced additional barriers to taking paid work. Those who had left the workforce to bring up their children had great difficulty getting jobs – a matter of particular concern for lone mothers who wanted to find work following the breakdown of their marriage. In part the difficulty stemmed from a loss of confidence.

I was divorced about four years ago, so I had to pick meself up, sort meself out and then get back into the working world . . . It's just to start me off and then when the kids are older I can go onto something bigger and better, but it's a big step for me to actually start working after ten years, you know, even doing one and a half hours, it's a start.

[Going to the Jobcentre] was so different, I can't really explain. It was like going to a different world. You know, 'cos you've been at home, you've been this little homemaker for years and then suddenly you're in the Jobcentre. It's so different I just couldn't hack it.

In other cases it was because women's skills were out of date or they lacked recent work experience. Pam was a lone parent who had taken a course in word processing in order to get a job. She had subsequently applied for a clerical job with her local council only to be turned down.

[There is] a lot of talk about women returners, especially in information technology, but it's all just completely vanished, it's like some sort of mirage. The first people to get wiped out are women.

There was also the problem of childcare. For some women, caring for their young children took precedence over working. But those who did want to work faced problems finding care for their children at a price they could afford, regardless of whether they lived in urban or rural areas.

Although women with younger children imagined they would be able to return to work when their children were old enough to go to school, in practice this was by no means so easy. Finding a job with hours that matched school hours was a headache, as was childcare during school holidays.

(Ford *et al*, forthcoming; Grant, 1995; Kempson *et al*, 1994; Shucksmith *et al*, 1995; Speak *et al*, 1995; Third, 1995.)

Retraining
Over the last 15 years there have been a number of government initiatives designed to help unemployed people to get jobs. The early schemes, such as the Training and Opportunities Scheme (TOPS), offered general skills training, while more recent initiatives have been targeted on the long-term unemployed and designed to deliver basic rather than skills training. Employment Training (ET) was introduced in February 1988 and, in April 1993, it was replaced by Training for Work. This is now the main training programme aimed at long-term unemployed adults. It is open to those aged 18–63 who have been registered unemployed for 26 weeks or more, although priority is given to unemployed people with disabilities and people who have been unemployed for more than

12 months. People participating in the Training for Work scheme (and its predecessor ET) are offered the opportunity to gain work experience and they receive £10 on top of their benefit payments.

Views about these schemes seemed to be mixed. A minority of unemployed people rejected them out of hand as an insult.

> *I mean it's an insult to offer somebody £10 a week on top of their dole money. I think it's a total insult. I mean I'd rather work for nothing. I'd rather do charity work.*

The research suggests, however, that most unemployed would prefer to do anything rather than sit at home not working. A man who had been made redundant from his job as a site manager for a major building firm welcomed the opportunity to use his skills again. He was offered the opportunity to supervise the restoration of an old farmhouse, which restored some of his self-esteem. Even so he felt 'used'. From his point of view he was a skilled worker, using his skills, but earning just £10 a week.

> *I felt used actually and, at the end of the day, I felt that I was being exploited personally . . . I thoroughly enjoyed it, it was interesting . . . But if that work had to be done, why couldn't it have been full-time.*

Many other trainees commented that the £10 they received on top of their benefit did not even cover the additional costs of going to work.

These schemes have had only a modest success. Many people fail to complete their training and only about a third of those who see it through to the end find full-time jobs. But this has to be seen in context, as the people recruited to the Training for Work scheme are drawn from the groups who are least likely to find work. Several studies identified instances where people had been through training schemes more than once and still had not found work.

Job Plan workshops were also introduced in April 1993. These last for one week and aim to help long-term unemployed people set goals and compete successfully for jobs and training programme opportunities. Those who do not attend forfeit their social security benefit. But while the research found a degree of support for the training schemes, there was little for the workshops. Participants felt that the workshops addressed the wrong issue – the problem they faced was too many people chasing too few jobs.

Well I got bullied into one of these restart courses last year. Absolute waste of time and money. People telling you things you already know . . . they're trying to teach you how to write a letter properly and all this . . . Most of us have been looking for jobs for over three years. It's pretty obvious we know how to write. It's just the employers don't know how to write back, even if it's saying no . . . Out of 90 job applications, you'd be extremely lucky to get five refusals.

(Ford *et al*, forthcoming; Kempson *et al*, 1994.)

Changing nature of jobs

Alongside high levels of unemployment, there has been a shift in the types of jobs on offer. Over the past 15 years there has been a considerable growth in part-time jobs, temporary work and self-employment. Often these are the only options available to someone who is looking for work, with the consequence that people who have been unemployed are over-represented among those in temporary or part-time jobs or low-paid self-employment.

Moreover, many of the jobs on offer are low-paid ones. Indeed, research for the *Inquiry into Income and Wealth* showed that hourly wages for the lowest paid were lower in real terms in 1992 than they had been in 1975. This affected workers of all ages, but it was especially so for young people (Gosling *et al*, 1994). The inquiry identified a number of reasons for the increase in low-paid jobs. First, technological changes have been raising the productivity of more skilled workers faster than that of less skilled ones and they are, therefore, able to command even higher wages in the labour market. Secondly, there is the declining influence of trade unions and wages councils. And finally, the impact of education on wage levels, especially for young people, is much greater now than even ten years ago (Joseph Rowntree Foundation, 1995).

Part-time employment
Few breadwinners were prepared to consider part-time jobs, especially if (as was often the case) they were also low paid. The main exceptions were skilled workers, especially those in white-collar work. Here, even a part-time job was seen as a way of getting a foot on the ladder.

For example, an unemployed plumber retrained as an HGV driver, but could only find a job working two days a week. Taking this was a gamble, as the amount he earned was less than he was getting in Income Support and assistance with his mortgage payments.

On a basic week, and with four to five hours of overtime, I was getting less than I was getting on Income Support. But I turned round and said to [my wife] 'Well, I'm in a rut and I've got to do something to get out of it. Now if I'm in this job and I'm earning less it's going to give me the incentive to look around for something better', which is what I did. I was on there for three months, we were struggling.

But it paid off as he subsequently found a job 'with a decent wage . . . the basic was £196'.

Generally the breadwinners who took part-time jobs could afford to do so either because they had children, and so qualified for Family Credit, or because their partner was also able to find work. In contrast, single people often thought they could not afford to consider unskilled, part-time working once they took account of the expenses they would incur. This was especially the case among home owners who, unlike tenants, receive no help with their housing costs if they work.

(Ford *et al*, forthcoming; Kempson *et al*, 1994; Morris and Ritchie, 1994; Shucksmith *et al*, 1995.)

Temporary jobs

Attitudes to temporary jobs were also divided. But they related less to skill levels than to housing tenure. Many unskilled workers, especially those in the building trade, had moved from one short-term job to another for years. White-collar workers, too, took temporary contracts in the hope that they would lead to permanent employment.

But people with mortgages needed to think twice before taking a temporary job. Unlike tenants, home owners do not receive help with their housing costs as soon as they become unemployed. Indeed, since October 1995 there has been a reduction in the help given with mortgage interest repayments in the early months of unemployment. Previously, unemployed mortgage holders received assistance with half of their repayments for the first 16 weeks but then were usually helped with the full amount. Now people who lose their job receive nothing for the first two months and then half payments for a further four months –provided their mortgage was taken out before October 1995. (More recent borrowers are in an even worse position, receiving no state assistance for the first nine months of unemployment.) This has made home owners very wary about taking a temporary job.

If it weren't for that I would've taken [a six-month job advertised at the Jobcentre] ... If they said if it doesn't work out or whatever you can go straight back onto the Income Support without losing your 13 weeks, then I would have been tempted.

In part, it was worry about falling further behind with their mortgage and, in part, a concern that their mortgage lender would not be so understanding next time round.

Even tenants were wary about temporary jobs, if they had previously experienced long delays while their housing benefit was worked out. The problems arising from delays have recently been tackled by the decision to continue paying full housing benefit for the first four weeks after claimants return to work.

I'm looking for something permanent. Temporary's no good 'cos you come, you go, you're on benefits then you come off them, you go back on them. Instantly you're suspended while they find out why you're not working any more. OK you might get that money back in three months' time, but that's three months you've got to make do without money and it can be as long as six months by the time it's sorted out. You can't live like that.

(Ford *et al*, forthcoming; Kempson *et al*, 1994; Morris and Ritchie, 1994; Shucksmith *et al*, 1995.)

Working in the informal economy

One consequence of the lack of full-time permanent jobs is the number of people who are apparently part of the 'informal economy' – that is working while claiming Income Support but not declaring their earnings. Social security law does permit claimants to work and to keep a set amount of their earnings on top of their benefit; after this it is deducted pound for pound. Lone parents and people out of work for two years or more can retain £15 a week; others £5. (There are plans to allow claimants to cumulate half of their 'disregard' and have the money paid to them in a back-to-work bonus.)

By and large claimants were aware of this current rule and many lone mothers, in particular, took advantage of it to supplement their benefit by regularly working a few hours a week. But competition for these very part-time jobs was fierce and they were often described as 'gold dust'.

> *I can't get anything. You'll always find these little cleaning jobs that you can actually do, because you're not allowed to earn more than £15 are you? These little cleaning jobs which are two or three mornings a week and you get, say, just under that. You can't get them – there are hundreds of people going after them.*

Others had regular jobs earning more than their 'disregarded' amount, only a minority of whom had declared their earnings. Generally speaking they worked in part-time jobs in order to pay off arrears they had built up on household bills, and the amounts they earned were not large. For example, the lone mother, described at the beginning of Chapter 3, took a job feeding cats because her financial situation was 'absolutely desperate'. Without these undeclared earnings she said that she 'would have felt like turning to crime'. By working and not declaring her income she was, ironically, committing a criminal offence. But it was need rather than greed that had led her to do it.

It was more common for people who claimed benefit and worked to take on casual jobs. This was most prevalent among unemployed men and the jobs available were usually very short-term – a day or two here and there. There would therefore have been little point in signing off benefit only to sign on again later in the week. More to the point, declaring the income would have defeated the whole purpose of working, since most people desperately needed the money.

Mark, for example, was buying his home on a mortgage when he lost his job. But the assistance he received with the repayments was £180 short of the £262 a month he was supposed to pay. He took any casual work he could find to avoid losing his home.

> *It's something that I don't like doing for fear of getting caught. It's only like in desperate situations I'd ever go into that. But there's lots of it about. I'm amazed – people coming up to you when they know you do that kind of thing.*

Many people said that casual work was widely available if you knew where to look. And this was as true in rural areas as it was in urban ones. Generally speaking these were cash-in-hand service jobs – gardening, building work, joinery, decorating, bar work, cleaning. The sums of money were up to £40–50 for a day's work, but people rarely got more than a day's work at a time.

(Kempson *et al*, 1994; Morris and Ritchie, 1994; Shucksmith *et al*, 1995.)

Low pay

The issue that caused widest comment among the people interviewed, however, was the low rates of pay offered by the jobs that were available.

Plenty of penny ha'penny jobs – you know for a hundred quid a week.

I don't consider the Jobcentre a legitimate place to go, it's more like a joke centre because of the wages on display down there. If a teenager wants £82 a week gross, that's fine on them, but I want that more than doubled.

I've talked to other HGV drivers and they're being paid £2.50 an hour . . . You know it's ridiculous the wages they're paying.

Wages of £2.50 an hour or less were not at all uncommon. For example, one man had been paid £150 for an 80-hour week as a security guard; another had earned £100 for a 45-hour week in a factory; a third had been offered three jobs since he had been unemployed – £109 for a 46-hour week as a hotel porter, £95 for a 40-hour week as a night watchman, and £75 for a full-time catering job. Wages at this level were almost the norm for women in manual jobs. Of two women working as care assistants, one had earned £110 a week working full-time and the other received £48 for a 20-hour week – the equivalent of £2.40 an hour. Two full-time shop assistants earned £89 and £70 a week respectively.

In part the objection to these rates of pay was a matter of self-esteem, but it was also a question of economics – as the discussion below shows.

Some breadwinners *did* take on these jobs, but only when they were able to top up their earnings in some way. Low hourly rates were accepted when there were opportunities for regular overtime. Low-paid jobs were also taken by people who would qualify for Family Credit – especially by women who were lone parents and who did not expect to earn more than £2–3 an hour. Men whose wives could also find work were likewise more prepared to take a job with low pay. Skilled manual and white-collar workers were meanwhile prepared to take a low-paid job in the hopes that it would lead onto something better. Indeed, there were many examples of unemployed people taking jobs paying less than their previous one. A former manager had earned £21,000 a year in his last job but, having been out of work for four years, was considering a job paying half that amount.

(Ford *et al*, forthcoming; Kempson *et al*, 1994; Morris and Ritchie, 1994; Shucksmith *et al*, 1995.)

Tackling low wages

There is a growing recognition of the need to tackle the problem of low wages. On the one hand this has focused on increasing the availability of in-work benefits – the government is launching a pilot scheme to test a new benefit, Earnings Top-up, to supplement low wages for single people and couples without children. On the other there is a debate not just about the need for a minimum wage but about the level at which it should be set.

In-work benefits

Few people understood in-work benefits very well, but they know enough to realise that they could well be caught in a poverty trap. This often deterred them from taking the jobs on offer.

> *The less you work the more the Social give you. If you earn £100 a week, they give you £50. If you earn £150, they'll only give you a tenner a week, so you're in the same boat all the time. There's no job that'll pay me enough to keep on top. There's so much I have to pay.*

Moreover, with the possible exception of lone mothers, people who were out of work wanted jobs that would take them off benefit altogether. Claiming benefit when they were not working was accepted as unavoidable. But if they worked they wanted to 'earn a decent living' and not to be subsidised by the State.

(Ford *et al*, forthcoming; Kempson *et al*, 1994; Third, 1995.)

Minimum wage

Most people contemplating low-paid work would, then, be happier with a wage that would cover their outgoings with a small amount of leeway. The qualitative research provides a wealth of information on the wages people would need. This includes:

• the amount that unemployed people calculate they need to earn to cover their outgoings

• the income level at which people do not feel they have to supplement their earnings

• the income level at which there is a low likelihood of problem debts.

Each of these calculations leads to remarkably similar sums of money. It would appear that single people need about £150 net income a week (but less if they are not householders); couples without children need £175 net; lone parents need £180 net; and couples with children need £200 net.

Calculations by people out of work
Most unemployed people had a fairly clear idea of how much they needed to live on. For example, a single man had, with the help of a Citizen's Advice Bureau money adviser, calculated that he needed £150 a week to cover all his bills and allow £20 a week for food. A lone mother with two children had worked out that, if she earned £180 a week, she could cover all her outgoings and still have £10 a week to put by for emergencies. A childless couple said that £180 a week would cover all their needs, except cigarettes and a social life. Another £20 a week would be needed for these. These figures, although illustrative, were typical of the replies given by others.

(Ford *et al*, forthcoming; Kempson *et al*, 1994.)

Earnings that need to be supplemented
It has already been seen that people were prepared to take part-time and low-paid jobs if they could supplement their earnings in some way. Tony, a foundry worker, earned £156 a week basic pay. To support himself, his wife and two children, he either worked the day shift with overtime, earning £180 a week, or he did the night shift, getting £220. Cheryl, a lone parent, worked as a residential care assistant for a basic wage of £110 a week. At this level she was entitled to Family Credit, but instead she regularly worked overtime to bring her wages up to £150 a week. Ken earned just £120 a week working in a factory. Unlike others he had no opportunities for overtime and so his wife also worked full-time as a shop assistant, taking home £77 a week. Again, this took them just above the Family Credit level.

(Ford *et al*, forthcoming; Kempson *et al*, 1994; Morris and Ritchie, 1994.)

Incomes needed to avoid financial difficulties
Finally, while there was no clear point at which people faced financial difficulties, it was apparent that on net incomes of £165–85 families with children had a 50 per cent likelihood of getting into arrears with basic bills. The more their earnings fell below this level, the greater their financial difficulties, and at £100 a week they were virtually certain either to have arrears on their basic household bills or to be going without food and other essentials to pay their bills.

(Kempson *et al*, 1994; Morris and Ritchie, 1994.)

Minimum wage level
In the debate about a minimum wage the figure of £4.15 an hour has been put forward by some trade unions, while others argue that it should be less than that amount. Setting aside the political arguments, evidence from the qualitative studies suggests that a wage of £4.75 an hour would be required to give incomes close to the amounts needed to cover outgoings and avoid financial difficulties. Even then, couples would need to supplement the earnings in some way (see Tables 6 and 7).

Such calculations, based on a 'family wage' approach, need to be used with some caution. Minimum wage debates are as much about equity in the labour market as about family poverty. Also many of those who would stand to gain most are part-time 'second-earners' and this could serve to further widen income inequalities. In reality, then, the most practicable solution may prove to be a combination of in-work benefits and a lower minimum wage than the calculations suggest.

Table 6 Net weekly incomes at a wage of £4.75 an hour, assuming a 40-hour week

	Single person	Couple without children	Lone parent with 2 children	Couple with 2 children
	£	£	£	£
Gross annual income	9880	9880	9880	9880
Personal tax allowance	3525	3525	3525	3525
Other tax allowances	–	1720	1720	1720
Taxable income	6355	4635	4635	4635
Less tax at 20%	640	640	640	640
Less tax at 25%	789	789	789	789
Less National Insurance	747	747	747	747
Net earnings	7704	8134	8134	8134
Plus Child Benefit	–	–	980	980
Plus One Parent Benefit	–	–	328	–
Net annual income	7704	8134	9442	9115
Net weekly income	148	156	182	175

Table 2 Net weekly incomes at a range of hourly rates, assuming a 40-hour week

| Rate per hour | Net weekly income (excl. in-work benefits) | | | |
	Single person	Couple without children	Lone parent with 2 children	Couple with 2 children
£	£	£	£	£
2.50	82	82	107	101
3.00	100	100	125	119
3.50	116	118	143	137
4.00	129	136	161	155
4.15	133	141	166	160
4.50	142	150	175	169
4.75	148	156	182	175

Increasing polarisation between two-earner and no-earner households

Married women's participation in the labour market grew quite markedly during the 1980s. And, while previously it was wives of relatively well-paid men who were most likely to work, wives of lower-paid men caught up over this decade.

Yet, over the same period, there was a growing polarisation between couples where both partners worked and those where neither had a job. Between 1975 and 1990, the proportion of couples who both worked increased from 51 to 60 per cent; while the proportion with no earner increased from 3 to 11 per cent. Not surprisingly, those with no earner were over-represented among the poorest 20 per cent of households (Gregg and Wadsworth, 1995). The qualitative research suggests three, partly interrelated, reasons for this polarisation.

First, there are factors that relate to the labour market. In general low-skilled manual workers tended to marry other low-skilled workers – indeed couples often met through work. As a consequence, double redundancies were not uncommon. In one study, three out of thirteen couples, where neither partner worked, had suffered a double redundancy. Having lost their jobs, both partners were looking for work in a very competitive job market.

Moreover, as previously seen, men were prepared to take a low-paid job when they could supplement the family income either by working overtime or when their wives, too, could get a job. Both wages were needed to meet the household outgoings. This was especially the case among low-waged home owners, who did not receive any assistance with housing costs. In such circumstances it was common for both partners to work.

Secondly, there are clear work disincentives arising from social security rules. It was very rare for women to be in work when their partners were unemployed, because the wages they could expect to receive were often lower than the amount they could get in social security payments. This particularly hit couples where the husband did not qualify for unemployment benefit, as Income Support entitlement is based on household rather than individual income. As a consequence there were explicit comments about work not being worthwhile for women in Income Support families, and instances where the wife had given up work when her husband became unemployed.

> *The wife would go out to work. She would go back where she was working before . . . the school. But if she goes back they'll take the money off me. It seems a silly policy as far as I can see. They're sort of telling you not to work. She'd only work an hour and a half a day, so it's not worth it.*

Again the impetus to do this was greatest for couples buying a home on a mortgage as, by the wife giving up her job, they became eligible for assistance with their mortgage interest payments. Subsequent changes to mortgage assistance rules, however, mean that they would now have to wait at least two months before receiving any help.

Work disincentives were increased because people who were out of work had low levels of understanding about in-work benefits – of Housing Benefit as well as Family Credit. When they calculated how much they would need to earn to cover all their expenses few people took in-work benefits into account. In some cases this was because they did not know, and could not find out, how much they might get, while others assumed they would get no help at all. This deterred women, in particular, from taking jobs, as their pay levels were likely to be even lower than their husband's and many of the jobs available were only part-time.

Thirdly, traditional values, of the man's role as breadwinner, were an important factor in many low-income households. Women who had been in low-paid unskilled jobs before having children frequently had a low attachment to the labour market and saw themselves, primarily, as mothers. In contrast, their husbands equated work with self-esteem and dignity and felt it was their role to provide for the family. They were very resistant to looking after the children while their wives went out to work. It was acceptable for the wife to work part-time and supplement her husband's low wages, but much less acceptable for her to become the breadwinner. The realities of the labour market acted to reinforce these views.

(Ford *et al*, forthcoming; Kempson *et al*, 1994; Morris and Ritchie, 1994; Shucksmith *et al*, 1995; Third, 1995.)

Summary

Increased job insecurity and a growth in part-time, temporary and low-paid jobs have made it more likely that some groups of people will become trapped on low incomes. There is now a substantial minority of the population for whom achieving a 'decent income' seems an impossible dream.

Among unskilled manual workers there is a high risk of getting into a downward spiral of increasing job insecurity and falling wage levels. Young people leaving school, those in their fifties, people in poor health or with disabilities, and women trying to return to the labour market all seem to fare badly in the current labour market – especially if they have limited skills.

Since low-skilled workers tend to marry other workers with low skills, these trends are magnified at the household level. This is demonstrated by the growing polarisation between households with two wage earners and those with none.

In recent years, government training schemes have been targeted on people caught in this downward spiral or who have been unemployed for long periods of time. But the real problems seem to lie elsewhere – in the education system and, above all, in the lack of jobs. Many participants in the training schemes see them as little more than shuffling the deck-chairs on the *Titanic*.

There is also a fairly widespread resistance to taking part-time, temporary and very low-paid jobs that would be inadequate to cover household bills. But people do take them if they are either skilled or white-collar workers and think it might lead onto a full-time permanent job, or they are unskilled and can see some other way of increasing their income – by working overtime or both partners in couples taking jobs.

In the course of the current debate, two distinct approaches have been proposed for tackling the problem of low pay – widening the availability of in-work benefits and setting a minimum wage. Using the qualitative research it is possible to shed further light on both of these issues.

First, there is clearly resistance to claiming in-work benefits. This, coupled with the widespread lack of knowledge about the benefits that already exist, does not auger well for any policy that relies upon them to overcome the problems of low pay.

Secondly, a minimum wage, even at the level being suggested by some trade unions, would not generate a level of income that would be sufficient to keep most households on a sustainable financial footing.

The inevitable conclusion appears to be that the only long-term solution is to expand the number of jobs so that everyone who is seeking employment has a reasonable expectation of finding a job that will provide a secure and adequate income.

5 Housing policy

Changes in the housing market have had a significant effect on the lives of low-income households. Shifts in tenure have restricted access to affordable rented housing. There has been a rise in homelessness and changes to subsidies have increased housing costs.

There have been long-term shifts in the pattern of housing tenure, with significant changes taking place in the past 15 years. Over the 1970s there was a fairly rapid decline in the number of people renting in the private sector, accompanied by increases in the numbers either buying a home on a mortgage or renting from their local authority. Since then there has been a policy of actively encouraging home ownership, while restricting new building by local authorities. These policies have had the effect of boosting the numbers of home buyers, while reducing the proportion of the population living in social rented housing. In recent years, there have also been attempts to revive the private rented sector, albeit at high rents.

Long-term increases in the level of homelessness have accelerated with the decline of affordable rented accommodation and the increase in mortgage possessions. This led to a rise in the numbers of families in temporary accommodation and to a growth in the numbers of single people living in hostels or, at the extreme, sleeping rough. Homelessness acceptances by local authorities have, however, fallen over the past few years.

As the importance of council housing declined, there have been fundamental changes to the nature of housing subsidies. Most notable of these has been the gradual erosion of 'bricks and mortar' subsidies for social rented housing, in favour of means-tested housing benefits for individuals.

While each of these changes has affected the lives of people living on low incomes in their own right, the overall effect has, in fact, been magnified by other socio-economic changes – especially shifts in the labour market discussed in Chapter 4.

Shifts in tenure

Government policy has influenced the relative supply of housing in each tenure and it is worth beginning by setting these out in some detail.

Successive post-war governments developed the role of local authorities as providers of rented accommodation to a point, in 1980, when one-third of all households lived in council housing. More recently that role has been restricted by the twin policies of allocating council housing only to those in need, while encouraging existing tenants to become home owners by giving them the right to buy their homes at a discount. This has been accompanied by a decline in new building so that there has been a marked reduction in local authority housing stock. There are more than a million fewer council homes available for rent now than there were 15 years ago.

At the same time there has been a greater emphasis on the role of housing associations as the main providers of new social rented housing, but this has by no means made good the shortfall in council housing. As a consequence there is a severe shortage of affordable rented housing.

Private renting, having continued to decline during the 1980s, has risen slightly in recent years; partly as a result of deregulation and partly through an increase in lettings by people unable to sell their homes. But such increases as have occurred tend to be short-term lets at high rents.

A number of factors have stimulated the large increase in home ownership. The Right to Buy and, to a much less degree, Rents to Mortgage schemes have encouraged well over a million council tenants to buy their homes since 1980. Over much the same period, deregulation of mortgage lending led to increased competition and a relaxation of lending criteria and further fuelled the growth in home ownership. Insufficient rented housing also meant that some people bought because their options were constrained. As a consequence many people living on relatively low incomes or in insecure employment bought a home over the 1980s. The recent recession hit these groups quite hard, resulting in many of them having their homes repossessed. Indeed, there are signs that, but for the Right to Buy, there would have been a fall in the level of home ownership in the past few years.

Access to social rented housing

The dramatic contraction in social rented housing (as a result of the Right To Buy scheme, coupled with a reduction in new building) means that access is now severely restricted. Indeed it has been estimated that at least another 90,000 homes a year may well be required to meet current needs – 117,000 if the backlog of unmet need is to be eradicated over the next 20 years. Production of social housing in the early 1990s has been running at 60,000 a year – well below the level needed (Holmans, 1995).

Long waiting lists

As a consequence waiting lists are long, and mainly people in 'priority need groups' are now accepted for rehousing by local authorities. Housing associations, too, are increasingly having to ration supply to people in greatest need.

The research shows that young couples without children faced very great difficulties getting a council home and those with very low incomes often started out living with parents or in temporary accommodation. In rural Scotland, for example, it was not uncommon for young couples to start their married lives in rented caravans or in 'winter lets'. Young people who realised that they had little prospect of either buying a home or of affording the rents in the private sector often put their names onto council waiting lists in their late teens. Patricia was living with her boyfriend in her parents' home. They would have liked to get married and set up on their own but could only afford to rent from the local authority, and they faced a very long waiting list.

> I'm really kicking myself for not putting my name down when I was 16 . . . I don't want to wait for the next seven years . . . But I'll put my name down now, and then in seven years, I mean, I don't know what's gonna happen in seven years. I could be unemployed. We both could be unemployed. We could have a couple of kids and we're out on the streets. So, I'll put my name down now and if a house does come up, well fine, but that's how long the waiting list is.

She knew that she would not be considered a priority unless she was either accepted as homeless or 'unless I'm pregnant, which I don't want to be to get a house. I mean, I plan to have a family some time in my life, but not now so I can get a house.'

Similar problems faced couples who had ill-advisedly bought a home. Those whose homes were repossessed as a result of mortgage arrears were generally only rehoused if they had young children. Couples without a family were not normally accepted for rehousing by either local authorities or housing associations. Most moved from one temporary home to another following the repossession.

Likewise, low-income couples without children who had negative equity on their homes often had such large shortfalls that the only long-term solution was to move into the social rented sector. They were seldom accepted onto waiting lists and they, too, moved into temporary accommodation, often staying with family or friends.

(Ford, 1994; Forrest *et al*, 1994; Shucksmith *et al*, 1995.)

Do teenage mothers queue jump?
This acute shortage of homes has fuelled concerns that young single women may be getting pregnant to jump the housing queue. The research, however, provides little evidence to support these views.

A study of young single mothers noted that there were two main routes to council housing – waiting lists and homelessness. The majority went down the waiting list route and had substantial waits before being allocated homes. None of them were housed within six months and waits of two years were fairly common. Homelessness was the route to housing in fewer than a third of cases.

It is possible that, when faced with very long waiting lists, some young mothers may collude with their parents to pretend they are about to become homeless. However, only one out of 31 young mothers admitted to this being the case and she had already been on the waiting list for 15 months.

> *They [the housing department] weren't doing owt. I'd been waiting for months, over a year, and there wasn't room like. Not really, 'cos me and [my sister] shared, so then there was three of us with the baby. In the end my mam said they'd have to give me a place 'cos it was getting her down as well, and my dad. So she wrote and told them that I couldn't stay no longer, that she'd turn me out. I don't think she would have, like, not really.*

Others who were classed as homeless when they took up their tenancies had almost all been on the waiting list and had fully intended to wait their turn. They were all living in temporary accommodation – living with friends or in hostel accommodation. None of them had used pregnancy as a means to independence. On the contrary, it had forced independence on the young women concerned.

(Burghes and Brown, 1995; Speak *et al*, 1995.)

Specific areas of shortfall
Attention often focuses on the *lack* of homes, but there are other consequences of a shrinking social rented sector which mean that suitable housing is not available even for those who would be considered a priority for housing.

There are, now, geographical inequalities in provision. Council homes in 'desirable' and rural areas were the ones most likely to have been bought under the Right to Buy scheme. In one rural district council of Northumberland 1,306 council properties had been bought since 1980, leaving 3,469 to meet local needs. Most of the remaining housing was in the two larger urban areas in the district, with little provision in the rural ones. No 'general needs' council housing had been built since 1981. Much the same had occurred in a second district council, where 2,895 properties had been sold leaving 8,506 council homes which, like the housing association provision, were predominantly in two towns. Yet both councils were areas of high unemployment, with high levels of need for affordable housing in both the rural and the urban areas.

The same problem was noted in rural Scotland. Most people accepted they would almost certainly have to move to their nearest town to find a home, but often they were not available there either.

> *Most of the council houses there [the nearest town] have been bought. Very few of them change hands, which means . . . you've got a problem.*

> *If they [young people] can get a council house, it will be where the council can find a house rather than where they actually need to have a house.*

Although more acute in rural areas, the same problems occurred in more desirable parts of towns and cities.

Another consequence of the Right to Buy scheme has been a shortage of three-bedroom family homes, since these were often the first to have been bought.

> *. . . most of the [council] . . . three-bedroomed houses are now sold. Most of the people living in them have bought them. So it doesn't leave an awful lot of houses.*

Moreover, because there has been so little new building, public housing supply has not been able to respond to the increase in the number of single person households that is a feature of demographic and social changes. This poses a particular problem for vulnerable people with special needs. For example, the scarcity of council housing in four urban local authorities (in London, the North and the South of England) made it difficult to find suitable homes for people with mental health problems or limited mobility.

The consequence of these shortfalls is that people who fall into 'priority need groups' – lone mothers, families with children whose homes had been repossessed and 'vulnerable' single people with mental health problems or disabilities – were often placed in unsuitable temporary accommodation.

(Burghes and Brown, 1995; Carlisle, 1996; Ford, 1994; Jones, 1995; Pleace, 1995; Shucksmith *et al*, 1995; Speak *et al*, 1995.)

Increasing polarisation between neighbourhoods

Running alongside the restrictions in access to social housing has been an increasing polarisation between neighbourhoods, with homeless families and other new tenants often offered accommodation on the least popular, hardest-to-let estates.

Over the 1980s, such estates housed an increasing proportion of unemployed people, children and young people, lone parents and, in London, ethnic minorities. Growing concentrations of 'disadvantaged' groups added to their already poor reputations. They became notorious for being not just impoverished, but dirty, vandalised, unrepaired, lacking facilities, cut off by lack of public transport, with high levels of crime. The difficulties of living on these estates has been described in Chapter 3.

Despite these trends, it has been possible to reverse the decline in some estates through intensive local management, responsive to the community's needs. A number of local authorities have adopted an approach to managing difficult estates in which:

- lettings, repairs and caretaking are controlled by local managers

- local managers are free to innovate

- strong political backing allows immediate action, cutting through red tape

- there is an open-door policy, encouraging tenants to voice their point of view and giving those views priority

- police are encouraged to return to the beat

- committed, locally based staff inspire confidence and generate action.

A long-term study of 20 of the most unpopular estates in the country showed how successful this approach could be. Fifteen years after the introduction of local management, residents on most estates believed that conditions had improved and both tenants and staff were enthusiastic about the locally based services that had evolved. The number of empty properties had fallen in proportion to the extent of local control over lettings. Levels of rent arrears had fallen – in some cases to below the average for the local authority. The estates were far cleaner and the repairs service had improved. The one exception to this trend was crime and disorder, which did not decrease with the general improvement in conditions.

These successes appeared to be due to prolonged efforts by staff and residents and not to a reduction in social problems, which had generally intensified. Residents' involvement was intrinsic to the success and, in most instances, tenants were far more involved in estate affairs than they had been 15 years previously. But there were limits to the role that tenants could play. The complexity of the problems being tackled meant that they needed training and continuing support.

Intensive localised management, involving a targeted multi-agency approach and full tenant participation could, however, be as effective in arresting the decline of estates as large-scale reinvestment.

(Power and Tunstall, 1995.)

Deregulation of the private rented sector

The government has sought a solution to shortages in social rented housing by stimulating the private rented sector. This it did through the Housing Act 1988, which introduced two new types of private tenancy for all new lettings by non-resident landlords. Rents on these assured and assured-shorthold tenancies are market rents, fixed between the landlord and the tenant. It is not possible for the tenant to apply to the rent officer for a 'fair' rent, which previously acted as a brake on rents. Nor can local authorities refer the rents of Housing Benefit claimants in the private rented sector to the rent officer.

These changes have helped to stimulate the recent modest growth in the private rented sector. Over half of the private rented housing stock in 1995 was property that had only been let since deregulation. But the slump in the home ownership market has also played a part, as one in ten private lettings are by people unable to sell their homes (Crook *et al*, 1995; Kemp and McLaverty, 1995).

Access for people living on low incomes
Deregulation of the private rented sector may have increased the supply of housing, but the high rents charged and the conditions attached to tenancies mean that few low-income households can consider renting privately. Many private landlords were found to specifically exclude people claiming social security.

> *I'd phoned round all the places in the paper up for rent, whatever. Some of them were good enough to state 'No DSS accepted'. But guaranteed, nine times out of ten, if you're not working, they're not interested.*

They also required new tenants to pay a deposit or rent in advance. The 1988 Housing Act made it legal for landlords to charge 'key money' (a non-returnable payment) and, if a letting agent was used, a fee usually had to be paid for the service. Each of these acted as a barrier to people on low incomes renting in the private sector. Even if rents were affordable with assistance from Housing Benefit, two-thirds of tenants were expected to make some form of advance payment – usually a deposit averaging £200 and advance rent of a further £230.

A number of local authorities and voluntary bodies have recently set up schemes to help people living on low incomes overcome these barriers, by offering cash or loans or arranging written guarantees for the landlord. Preliminary research findings suggest that they had a high degree of success in helping clients to move into self-contained flats or houses.

(Kemp and McLaverty, 1995; Rugg and Sanderling, forthcoming.)

Rents and Housing Benefit restrictions
Deregulation has allowed rents in the private sector to increase and raised questions about the extent to which Housing Benefit should subsidise private tenants. Local authorities have long had the power to restrict the rent eligible for Housing Benefit if they felt that it was too high or the property too large, but these rent rises brought the question of 'reasonable rents' into even sharper focus.

Concerns have been expressed that people eligible for Housing Benefit do not try to negotiate rent reductions or look for cheaper properties. But research suggests these are unfounded. Difficulties finding accommodation, not a lack of shopping around, seemed to be the reason why claimants took on properties at high rents. Compared with others, tenants whose rent had been restricted had more problems finding somewhere to rent and had looked at many more properties.

Moreover, many tenants *had* tried to negotiate a lower rent with the landlord but, with high levels of housing demand, were generally unsuccessful. Others had worried that they might lose the property altogether if they started haggling.

> *Well, I don't think you can really negotiate, like. It's alright saying negotiate but you might be told just to go and get some place else mightn't you? . . . I mean they usually say a rent and they stick to it don't they?*

Most tenants had no idea how much Housing Benefit they would get and even when they approached the local housing department for further information they had not been given any guidance. So, when they took on an expensive property, they had little idea how much of the rent they would be left to find themselves.

> *I did try and find out from the rent people whether I would be able to obtain benefit and, if I could, what sort of rent I should be looking at and what I would be able to get paid. But they couldn't and/or wouldn't tell me.*

> *I asked them, but they said they can't tell you. They say 'You'll have to put in a claim and then we'll see.' So that means I could move in somewhere and then have to move out again because they won't pay the full rent.*

Tenants who faced the prospect of having their Housing Benefit reduced because their 'eligible rent' was set below the amount they had to pay had three options open to them: to find the difference themselves; to try to negotiate a lower rent; or to move into cheaper accommodation. In practice the second and third options were rarely open to them and most struggled to find the additional rent out of low incomes.

When she separated from her husband, a lone parent moved with her two children into a three-bedroom flat. She borrowed £400 to cover the deposit and advance rent so that she could get the tenancy. However, the flat was in a poor state of repair and the council decided only to pay £35 Housing Benefit, leaving her to make up the remaining £15 of her £50 a week rent. As she was living on Income Support, this put a real strain on her household budget and she got into arrears with her gas and electricity bills. She tried working part-time, but after meeting the costs of childcare she was no better off. In the end she stopped making up the rent and looked for somewhere else to live. She found a smaller flat with two bedrooms, for which the council was, ironically, happy to meet £60 of her £65 rent.

As one of a 'protected group' she should not, in fact, have had a restriction applied to her rent at all. From January 1996, however, even 'protected' tenants (families with children and disabled or elderly people) will be subject to such restrictions on their rent.

(Kemp and McLaverty, 1995.)

Insecurity and disrepair
Although deregulation has made it easier for people who cannot sell their homes to rent them to others, several studies have highlighted the insecurity of tenure and disrepair that their tenants can face. Home owners who rented out their homes in this way were often in financial difficulties themselves. Their properties were frequently in a poor state of repair and, where they had run up mortgage arrears, their tenants faced the prospect of being evicted if the property was repossessed. Because many of these landlords were more amenable to people claiming benefit, such difficulties were more likely to have been experienced by low-income tenants.

(Kemp and McLaverty, 1995; Shucksmith *et al*, 1995; Speak *et al*, 1995.)

Problematic home ownership
Although house prices and mortgage rates have fallen over the early 1990s, home ownership still remains beyond the reach of most people on low incomes, especially as mortgage lenders have tightened their lending criteria.

Rural areas
The affordability of home ownership in rural areas has been exacerbated by the influx of commuters and people buying second homes. Their move to the countryside has pushed house prices up beyond the reach of young people and other low-income local people.

> *There's houses have been on the market up here . . . but generally they've been expensive to buy and it's the competitive element. You are up against people buying from down south.*

> *I think it's very hard for young people here to get a house, to own their own house, because the prices are so huge . . . It's very difficult for young people on a lowish wage, or even a medium wage, to be able to afford any of the houses here.*

The effects on local people are well illustrated by a young crofter on the Isle of Harris who was living with his parents. When the house on the croft came up for sale, he wanted to buy it but a family from outside the area offered a price that was way beyond his reach. Eventually, he moved to a caravan in the next township, while the croft house was only used for a month a year for holidays.

(Shucksmith *et al*, 1995.)

Low-income home buyers
The shortage of social housing, coupled with the high costs of renting in the private sector, have persuaded people to buy homes even when they have low incomes or risk unemployment.

For example, when Helen split up from her partner the house they had owned was sold. She tried to get a council home near her family, upon whom she relied for childcare. However, she was told that she would have a five-year wait and was offered a place in a hostel some distance away from her family. She felt she had no other option but to buy a home and found a former council house at the bottom of the market. But, having no earned income, she had problems getting a mortgage and ended up signing a contract which permitted repossession if she defaulted on a single payment.

Patricia and her boyfriend, faced with a probable seven-year wait for a council home were also considering buying a home, despite the fact that only Patricia had a job – as a shop assistant. Her boyfriend, a painter-decorator, was looking for work.

(Jones, 1995; Shucksmith *et al*, 1995.)

Mortgage arrears and possessions
For people in low-paid or insecure jobs, home ownership was often unsustainable in the medium- to long-term and they ran a high risk of falling behind with their mortgage payments.

In fact, the rapid rise in mortgage arrears and possessions over the early 1990s was concentrated among people living on low incomes. Even those who had bought at a discount through the Right to Buy scheme were not immune from this trend. In some cases the mortgage had never been sustainable from the outset, but most people had fallen into arrears because they experienced a drop in their income – through job loss, small business failure or a fall in earnings.

When I first bought it there was money around. But then I got laid off, so I was actually signing on when I first bought it, about six months afterwards.

A couple in their late fifties had been one of the first households to exercise their Right to Buy – in 1980. At that time they were both in secure jobs that were fairly well paid, but both had lost their jobs in the recession of the early 1990s.

I was a site manager, building houses . . . and it seemed a darn good thing to do with the discount we got as council tenants . . . We're up for sale now . . . we don't think, if I don't go to work on some sort of salary, that we will be able to hang onto this place . . . I mean if we had a choice we'd stay here wouldn't we?

Such problems are far from over. After an initial decline, the number of repossessions has recently started to rise once again. There were 25,200 repossessions in the first half of 1995 and in June 1995, 401,750 households were in arrears of three or more months with their mortgage. Since 1990 about 300,000 households have had their home repossessed, with the numbers peaking in 1991, when 75,540 properties were taken into possession. Changes in the extent to which mortgage interest payments of unemployed home owners' mortgage payments are protected by Income Support seem likely to increase the incidence of both mortgage arrears and possessions in the future.

(Ford, 1994; Ford *et al*, forthcoming; Herbert and Kempson, 1995; Kempson *et al*, 1994.)

Negative equity
Widespread negative equity, affecting at least a million home owners, has been a further consequence of the recent recession.

Although most common in white-collar households, it was those in social classes C2 and E who had the highest levels of negative equity relative to the value of their home. There was, moreover, a group of households on low or insecure incomes who lived in less saleable properties and who seemed likely to have problems for the foreseeable future.

Frequently households with negative equity also had a high risk of falling into arrears with their mortgage payments. As a consequence many who had their homes repossessed were left with a large debt outstanding – often running into tens of thousands of pounds.

It is quite clear that, in these circumstances, home ownership can become a route into long-term poverty.

(Ford, 1994; Forrest *et al*, 1994.)

Increases in homelessness

Homelessness has always affected a minority of households who, because they have low incomes, cannot find a home they can afford. But since the early 1960s there has been an upward trend in homelessness. Official statistics show that the numbers of households accepted as homeless by local authorities accelerated over the late 1980s and reached a peak in 1991 and 1992. During these years around 180,000 households were accepted for rehousing in Britain – almost double the number ten years previously. Since then the numbers have fallen very slightly.

These figures do *not* include people who have not been accepted as statutory homeless – mostly single people, but also non-pensioner couples without children. Although there have been various attempts to provide figures for the numbers of people in these categories, there are still no reliable national statistics of either homelessness generally or the numbers living on the streets.

At first, the increase in homelessness was limited to London and then to other major cities. It is now a national problem which few communities escape.

The causes of homelessness

The chief cause of homelessness is the shortage of affordable housing and, as such, it is primarily a problem that affects people on low incomes. Limited access to social rented housing and high rents on the one hand, and tenure insecurity in the private sector and risky home ownership on the other, have all played a part in the growth of homelessness. But so, too, have factors such as relationship and family breakdown, which, as already seen, are often exacerbated by living on a low income.

Statutory homelessness

Local authorities have a duty to house families with dependent children, elderly people and those considered 'vulnerable' because of physical or mental disabilities – provided they are unintentionally homeless. In practice, most of those accepted by local authorities as statutorily homeless are families with children, including substantial numbers of lone parents. Young families, minority ethnic groups and people who are unemployed are all over-represented among those accepted.

Despite the fact that local authorities have a duty to house people in these groups, rehousing is not always automatic or smooth. People considered to be 'intentionally' homeless may not be housed at all. Research shows that this has been a particular problem for people with mortgage arrears who surrendered their homes before the lender obtained a court order. Many local authorities were unwilling to offer housing to such households and they often moved from one temporary address to another. Having to wait for a court order meant people had to meet lenders' legal costs *and* it caused a great deal of additional anxiety at a time that was already stressful enough.

> *There was a lot of uncertainty. We knew the building society would take possession, but we couldn't be sure of the council until it happened.*

People worried about whether they would literally be on the street; whether they would be able to move to somewhere with all their furniture or would need to store it; about being able to get their children to school; and even whether they would be able to keep pets with them.

Actual homelessness placed a strain on otherwise stable families, disrupted their children's schooling and took a toll on people's health.

A shortage of social rented housing meant that, in many areas, even those who were accepted as homeless were not always provided with a permanent home right away. Besides families with children, this included single 'vulnerable' people: people with mental health problems, people leaving care and young people who were considered 'at risk'. Many spent several months living in hostels before moving into unfurnished council flats. The scarcity of housing also meant that little account was taken of individual requirements resulting from people's disabilities.

The likelihood of being placed in temporary accommodation varied according to locality. Lone mothers in Newcastle, for example, were generally allocated a permanent home without first living in bed and breakfast or a hostel. In contrast, those living in rural Northumberland had a very high likelihood of being placed in temporary accommodation or the homeless families unit for, on average, about 4–6 weeks. It was quite common for mothers in these circumstances to give up and move in with friends or family, as the isolation and lack of support networks caused too great a strain. Those who did wait their time were eventually made one offer of housing. If they refused that offer they were placed at the bottom of the waiting list, unless they could prove that the property was unsuitable. In practice, few young mothers had the confidence to challenge the suitability of the housing offered and they took whatever was accepted. As a consequence many were housed in less desirable areas:

Why do they put us all here? They think it don't matter . . . just 'cos we're young. They don't treat you like proper families, just bung us down here. No-one wants to live down here.

and in properties in poor condition:

It were damp and there were cockroaches. It was disgusting. I told them but they just said, 'You accepted it'. Honest, it weren't fit for a dog, let alone a bairn. And all round the windows the wood was rotten so the rain came in.

. . . disgusting! It were a right bloody mess. The wallpaper were hanging off and the doors were all smashed. And it were filthy, really filthy.

Similar difficulties were reported by families who had been accepted as homeless following mortgage repossession in Luton or Bristol. Here the first move was generally into temporary accommodation – usually bed and breakfast – where they stayed for periods of between one and five months. And, when they were offered a home it was, again, in poor housing in undesirable neighbourhoods.

We were in B and B for nine weeks and then they offered us this house straight afterwards. It was uninhabitable. I wanted to get the papers in . . . there'd been squatters in who'd gutted the place. But, if I'd have turned it down we'd have gone to the bottom of the list and had to stay in bed and breakfast.

The area is not a good one to raise children. Kids start fires and race cars up and down – it's a rough estate.

Because of these problems, families often applied for transfers to better homes and neighbourhoods. But, in some local authorities, rehousing presented greater problems than getting a home in the first place.

(Carlisle, 1996; Ford, 1994; Pleace, 1995; Roaf and Lloyd, 1995; Speak, 1995.)

Single homelessness

Many young people leave home and, with support from their family or friends, succeed in setting up home without too many problems. But the risks of homelessness were found to be greatest for young people from low-income families, especially where they had been forced to leave home by family breakdown. Stepchildren, in particular, had an increased risk of being forced to leave home because of family disagreements.

Polly left home to get away from a stepfather who had abused her, physically, for a number of years.

I was always battered when I was younger. From about the age of seven my dad hated me, because I was'nae his daughter. I used to get battered, I used to go to school with a broken nose or bruises all over my body . . . And then my dad hit my mum.

Sandra and Janice had both left their homes because they had alcoholic fathers.

He used to hallucinate and run about wi' knives and things like that, and we always used to ask her to put him out. But she never would keep him out for any length of time. He always got coming back.

When Sandra and her sister had both moved out, their mother eventually told their father to leave. They then both moved back home. Janice was not so fortunate. After leaving home, she had been joined by her younger sister, whom she was trying to support.

I told [my sister] she would need to go up tae social security, she would need to get some sort of money. I mean I can afford to, like, feed her and that kind of thing, but I cannae afford to give her money . . .

Young people often (like Sandra and her sister) moved out for a relatively short period of time. But the ones who were not able to return home frequently embarked on a career of homelessness. In some cases they had a permanent home for a short period first; in others homelessness began as soon as they left home. One 16-year-old woman had left home because she did not get on with her parents. During the five months since she had moved out she had lived briefly with her boyfriend, but left when they split up. She then slept rough for over a month (in winter) until the police helped her find accommodation in a young person's accommodation project.

Another young woman, aged 18, had been the subject of a care order because of sexual abuse at the age of three. She remained in care for 12 years and said she was evicted when she was 16. She slept rough for more than six months and then moved into a young person's hostel. She 'had to move on' from there to an accommodation project. That, too, broke down as she 'did not get on with the people there'. This was followed by another two months of rough sleeping and a progress through at least five more accommodation projects, leaving either because she did not get on with the other people or because she broke the rules.

When she was interviewed she was living in a hostel, which her social worker had helped her to find.

These are extreme examples, which illustrate the problem at its worst. But they do demonstrate the problems faced by young people who, having had to leave home, are unable to get a secure foothold in the housing market.

As already seen in Chapter 3, there was a clear link between homelessness and poor health, which was at its most acute among people sleeping rough. In addition, homelessness and unemployment all too often went hand-in-hand. Young homeless people could not get a home because they did not have a job; and they could not get a job because they were homeless. And those without a permanent address were further disadvantaged by the problems they faced trying to claim Income Support. It is now recognised that this 'no home – no job; no job – no home' poverty cycle has to be broken and there is a growing number of initiatives trying to tackle the problem.

One such initiative was the establishment of seven pilot 'foyers', the aim of which was to provide an integrated approach to young people's housing and employment problems. Five of these schemes were based in existing YMCAs, the other two were purpose-built by housing associations. On the whole these schemes were judged a success. They reached young people who would not have used more formal employment services. And most participants both appreciated the support and respect they received from the staff and preferred the foyer approach to the more government programmes. The evaluation of the pilot concluded that 'reliable, integrated funding mechanisms – for revenue as well as capital – would be required to sustain a network of foyers in the longer term.' But, unfortunately, the pilot did not identify an obvious funding framework.

The problem of single homelessness tends to focus on young people, but older people leaving institutions faced similar problems. A study of ex-offenders showed that over half of them lost their homes while they were in prison. Those who had owned a home or had rented in the private sector almost invariably did so. Only social tenants who were in prison for less than a year seemed likely to retain their home.

Part of the problem lay in the fact that prison housing officers seldom considered the need to help prisoners *retain* their home – they tended to focus, instead, on helping them *find* housing when they were released. Secondly, the benefits system did little to help them to keep their home. Home owners received no help with their mortgage payments while they were in prison and all ended up having their homes repossessed. Tenants, then, received Housing Benefit for a year. It has since been reduced to 13 weeks, making it likely that social tenants, too, will now end up losing their homes.

A particular problem was faced by lone parents, whose children were taken into care while they were in prison. On release they should have been considered a priority case for rehousing. But they were caught in a Catch 22. They were not allocated housing because their children were in care and could not get their children out of care until they had housing.

(Anderson and Morgan, forthcoming; Anderson and Quilgars, 1995; Bines, 1994; Carlisle, 1996; Griffiths, 1995; Jones, 1995; Pleace, 1995; Roaf and Lloyd, 1995; Speak, 1995.)

People with special needs

A number of studies have highlighted the problems faced by single homeless people who are considered 'vulnerable', but who do not necessarily qualify for rehousing. Almost half of single homeless people in hostels and seven out of ten people sleeping rough had been in at least one form of institution. These included people leaving children's homes, psychiatric hospitals, alcohol or drug units, prison or young offender's institutions. Most of them had special needs.

We have already seen that the most common first move for single people facing homelessness was into temporary accommodation – usually a hostel. Such moves were not always welcome, particularly by people who wanted to 'go straight' or to avoid drugs. What they wanted most was a place of their own, but they faced a number of obstacles to making this a reality.

Like others, they had problems finding suitable accommodation to rent and sorting out Housing Benefit applications. In addition, many needed practical help and support to live independently. Despite considerable help in setting up their homes, young single mothers who had spent time in supported mother and baby hostels needed long-term support.

> I wanted to leave [the hostel], couldn't wait me. But when you're on your own it's different. No one to talk to all the day, no money and all that. At least here [mother and baby hostel] there's other mams and you can put the bairn down and know someone else will watch on like for a few minutes. Yeh . . . it's hard if you don't have no-one. That's why I'm back here all the time, can't bloody get rid of me now!

Similar feelings of vulnerability were expressed by single people with health and drug or alcohol-related problems who lived in hostels.

I would like a flat of my own, but I don't know whether I could handle it or not, the reasons being I'm an alcoholic and I'm a diabetic as well . . . So, I'm just thinking, you got a flat there, you're on your own.

Many people with special needs needed practical as well as emotional help. They needed advice and assistance with housekeeping, with money management and, depending on their circumstances with baby or health care. Hostel and housing workers often did all they could, but were limited by lack of resources and training. Frequently, people with special needs required the services of more than one agency, yet there was often a lack of integrated community care. Where such help was lacking, housing arrangements often broke down.

(Bines, 1994; Carlisle, 1996; Etherington *et al*, 1995; Ford, 1994; Griffiths, 1995; Jones, 1995; Pleace, 1995; Roaf and Lloyd, 1995; Speak *et al*, 1995.)

Changes in housing subsidies

Over the past 15 years, successive governments have implemented important changes in housing subsidies, with the aim of reducing overall costs. These have affected both tenants and home buyers, although they have done so in different ways with different consequences.

Tenants
Since 1980, there has been a shift from 'bricks and mortar' subsidies to means-tested personal benefits. In the local authority sector, general housing subsidy has been reduced to a point where it is only paid to a minority of local councils. The housing association sector continues to receive subsidies, through the Housing Association Grant (HAG). But the government has reduced the level of HAG in stages, from 75 to 62 per cent, and intends to reduce it further to 55 per cent.

Ironically, these changes took place over a period when the economic mix of tenants was narrowing to include a greater proportion of tenants either out of work or in low-paid employment. The argument for bricks and mortar subsidies is, therefore, stronger today than it was 15 years ago when there were more better-off council tenants.

The consequence of this shift has been a move towards market rents in the social rented sector, with rises ahead of inflation. Between 1989 and 1993 rents increased by 80 per cent for housing association assured tenancies, 60 per cent for council tenants, and 40 per cent for housing association fair rents. This has drawn more tenants into the remit of Housing Benefit and increased both the unemployment trap, where people are no better off in work than unemployed, and the poverty trap, where those who are in work are no better off if they increase their hours and earnings (Wilcox, 1994 and 1995).

Unemployment trap

Several studies have shown how tenants were quite confused about in-work benefits such as Housing Benefit. Few of those who were not working had any idea how much help they would get with their rent if they took a low-paid job. When they considered the wages on offer, they often assumed that they would need to cover their rent in full. So the higher their rent, the more they thought they would need to earn. This acted as a deterrent to lone mothers looking for work, like Rita who before having her three children had been a shop assistant.

> *I would have to think about paying £35 rent, poll tax, £10 a week school dinners . . .*
> *So I mean it would have to be a pretty executive wage to keep me going.*

And it made others more likely to turn down low-paid jobs.

(Ford *et al*, forthcoming; Kempson *et al*, 1994; Third, 1995.)

Housing Benefit poverty trap

The effect of means-tested in-work benefits, such as Housing Benefit, is such that large increases in earnings are needed to make any significant impact on net income levels. For households without children, the combined effect of Housing Benefit and Council Tax withdrawal (known as the taper) and tax and National Insurance deductions can leave just 10p disposable income from each additional £1 of gross earnings. For low-waged families with children, the effect is more marked still. The interplay between Family Credit and Housing Benefit can leave them with as little as 3p from each additional £1 they earn. Yet very high earners only face a marginal tax rate of 40 per cent.

The impact of the poverty trap on tenants' decisions regarding work was minimised by their very low levels of knowledge. But the minority who did understand how the taper worked felt that it was unjust. Colin was one of these and, as he had a young family, he was eligible for Family Credit in addition to Housing Benefit and Council Tax Benefit. This put him on the steepest taper.

The less you work, the more the Social give you. If you earn £100 a week, they give you £50. If you earn £150, they'll only give you a tenner a week. So really you're in the same boat all the time.

(Ford *et al*, forthcoming; Kempson *et al*, 1994; Third, 1995.)

Home buyers

The main subsidy for home buyers is tax relief on mortgage interest, known as MIRAS (Mortgage Interest Relief At Source), which has been progressively reduced with the long-term aim of abolishing it altogether. Most of these reductions have affected low-income home buyers.

The first step was to hold the limit for tax relief to the first £30,000 of the mortgage, at a time when prices were rising substantially. Then the government restricted tax relief to the standard rate of tax only – 33 per cent, later falling to 25 per cent. From 1994/5 tax relief fell 20 per cent and in 1995/6 it fell again to 15 per cent. In the absence of a mortgage benefit to assist low-waged home buyers with housing costs, they have felt the full brunt of these changes in higher mortgage repayments. Unlike tenants, home buyers only receive state help with housing costs if they are out of work. Hence, rising mortgage costs have exacerbated the unemployment trap.

Even with relatively low mortgage repayments of £262 a month, Mark could not afford to take the jobs advertised at his local Jobcentre.

I was actually applying for jobs before I was made redundant. The wages they was offering, there was no way I could survive on them. They wouldn't even cover the mortgage.

(Ford *et al*, forthcoming; Kempson *et al*, 1994.)

Summary

Most people living on low incomes are adequately housed. But there have been important changes in the housing market, which, together, have made it more difficult for people on low incomes to find and retain suitable housing at a price they can afford.

The limited availability of council and housing association properties, rising private rents following deregulation, and the substantial numbers of home buyers who have had their homes repossessed since 1990, have all contributed to a growing problem of homelessness.

The move towards market rents, as a result of the withdrawal of subsidies for social rented housing and rises in private sector rents following deregulation, has increased both the unemployment trap and the Housing Benefit poverty trap for tenants.

In the main, these changes have had the effect of making life for those living on low incomes more difficult than previously. Shifts from bricks and mortar subsidies to personal means-tested benefits have made it difficult for people to escape from poverty. And, for a minority of people who have had their homes repossessed with negative equity, home ownership has acted as a route into poverty and indebtedness. Low-income households were encouraged into home ownership but, for many, the dream has turned into a financial nightmare from which there is little prospect of escape for many years.

6 Consumer credit and household utilities

A basic tenet of recent government policy has been the belief that market forces offer the best means of achieving efficiency, low prices and consumer satisfaction. As a consequence, policies of deregulation and privatisation have been pursued wherever possible. The previous chapter considered the impact of these policies in the housing market. This chapter examines two further areas of expenditure that often account for a significant proportion of the household budgets of people on low incomes: consumer credit and the household utility companies (gas, electricity, water and telephones).

Consumer credit

The 1980s saw a credit boom following major changes in the financial services industry, which relaxed controls on credit and widened its availability. Various forms of credit control were used almost continuously up to the 1980s. Successive governments restricted borrowing for 'non-priority' purposes by regulating the balance sheets of financial institutions, and controlling the terms for consumer credit lending. These controls were lifted in 1980 and 1982 respectively. This was followed by relaxation of controls over the building societies in 1986, permitting them to offer a wider range of financial products, and again in 1988, allowing them to increase the proportion of funds raised from sources other than their investors.

At the same time, developments in risk assessment tools meant that the credit industry was able to widen its customer base to include many people on modest incomes.

Together, these changes paved the way for greater competition between financial institutions; for new entrants into the consumer credit market; for the development of new consumer credit products; and for the wider availability of credit to people who previously would have found it difficult to obtain.

Use of credit
As a result, a much wider cross-section of the public now has credit commitments than was the case 15 years ago. But although credit is used about equally regardless of income, the reasons for borrowing and the types of credit used varies quite markedly.

Earlier research showed that higher-income households tended to use a wide range of types of credit to promote a consumer lifestyle, while low-income households tended to borrow for necessities and from a much more restricted range of sources (Berthoud and Kempson, 1992).

From the qualitative research, however, it is possible to identify four fairly distinct ways that people on low incomes use credit:

- for consumer goods

- for household goods and necessities

- to smooth peaks and troughs in income

- to pay bills and other debts.

Consumer goods
Access to credit has allowed many people, living on modest earned incomes, to spread the costs of acquiring consumer goods and second-hand cars that they might otherwise have had to forgo.

> *We only have one thing at a time. We started with the washing machine. When we finished paying for that, we had the TV and video. We've decided next time we're going to have a deep freeze.*

These goods were most commonly bought using hire purchase and finance house loans, although loans from moneylenders were also used in this way. A study of moneylenders' customers showed that a third of them were borrowing to buy consumer goods.

Household goods and necessities
Similarly, by using credit, people on low incomes are able to spread the costs of buying basic household goods and necessities, such as cookers, washing machines, as well as smaller items of household equipment like towels, bedding and kitchenware. Those setting up home, whether as couples or as lone parents, often had little option but to buy on credit. We saw in Chapter 3 that young people faced costs of up to £2,000, to buy the most modest household furniture and equipment. Even buying second-hand, the costs, at £700, would have been beyond their reach without borrowing any money at all.

Credit was also relied on to replace major household appliances when they broke down, since few people had savings they could call upon in an emergency.

I had to buy that cooker, because they came round one night, there was a gas leak and they condemned it, the cooker. So, overnight, I had that. I had to get a new cooker on credit. I was forced to get that cooker, I didn't want to buy it.

In general, people used mail-order catalogues and hire purchase arranged through fuel boards to buy these goods, although moneylenders and doorstep traders were used too. Indeed, this was one of the most common reasons why people started to use such lenders.

Kettles, toaster, household things I wouldn't be able to afford, which is nearly everything . . . The kids' clothes, shoes. It probably costs a few pennies more than it would in the shop, but it's worth it in the end because you don't have to pay the outright cash, you see, you don't feel the pinch.

Children's clothes and baby equipment were other major areas of credit use, with mail-order catalogues being used in the main. From the start, parents wanted the best for their children and not to rely on hand-ons.

I'd love to go to Mothercare and just buy all that lovely stuff you see. She'd [baby daughter] look right good in all that bright coloured stuff and them little dungarees and that. I get a lot from my sister's club for her, it's the only way I can afford.

As children grew older, the importance of wearing the 'right clothes', to avoid bullying, persuaded mothers to buy their children's clothes from catalogues. At Christmas, parents relied on credit to buy their children presents – again often buying goods from mail-order catalogues.

Smoothing income fluctuations
Credit provided a means of smoothing the peaks and troughs of daily living expenses for those who lived on incomes that were both low and liable to fluctuations, depending on the availability of overtime or shift working. People also used credit to tide them over between jobs.

Overdrafts and credit cards fulfilled that function for people who had access to them – generally those in work.

This is why I've had to have an overdraft, just to help survive really, not for luxuries, not for holidays and things. That's all had to go by the by now. It's for living, just the basics.

When you're on a strict budget it can help. We tend to use credit cards to pay [unexpected expenses] and pay it back as quickly as possible.

But poorer people tended to prefer the control that one-off loans gave them. This generally meant borrowing from a moneylender or pawnbroker.

Paying bills

Credit also provided a lifeline for people who were unable to pay their bills – especially if they were being threatened with court action or disconnection from their fuel or water supply. While some people used credit cards or overdrafts for this purpose, it often meant getting a loan from a moneylender or pawnbroker. A study of licensed moneylenders found that lone parents and, more surprisingly, pensioners were especially likely to borrow money for this reason, although most people knew where they could go for a loan in an emergency.

Some people used moneylenders as part of a planned approach to managing their money. An elderly divorcee had started to use a moneylender to give her a degree of financial security and independence. When she was first separated, she had run up arrears on a number of household bills and had had to turn to her daughters for help. She wanted to avoid getting so dependent on her children again and so contacted her local moneylender.

I don't go out and spend it recklessly. If there's nothing I want, I put it in the bank. It's more of a security thing, really. I pay all my bills through that.

This controlled use was more common among older customers. In young low-income families with children, finances were often not nearly so easy to plan. Once they started borrowing to pay bills, it soon led them into deeper financial difficulties.

I think, 'how am I going to manage 'til next week now?' You sort of have to borrow to manage to next week and then next week you pay it back, and you ain't got enough to last you the week so you've got to borrow again, and it's like a vicious circle.

(Herbert and Kempson, 1995; Herbert and Kempson, 1996; Kempson *et al*, 1994; Morris and Ritchie, 1994; Rowlingson, 1994; Speak *et al*, 1995.)

Dual credit market

Not everyone has benefited equally from the wider availability of credit, and there is evidence of a dual credit market. People in work (even low-paid work) could select from a wide range of relatively low-cost credit sources. Those living on social security frequently had their access to commercial credit limited to the more expensive sources such as moneylenders, doorstep traders or pawnbrokers. Mail-order catalogues were the only type of credit that cut across this dual market, being used as frequently by people living on social security as they were by people in work.

The reasons for this market segmentation lie partly in the ways that commercial creditors assess credit-worthiness and partly in consumer choice.

High street lenders screen potential customers using a combination of credit referencing and credit scoring. The first of these takes account of the applicant's personal details, especially their past history of borrowing and arrears. The second is a statistical technique which assesses, for a given set of personal and financial characteristics, the likelihood that an applicant will default on a credit commitment. Other than a large number of current arrears or recent county court judgements, no single factor would lead to an applicant being turned down. But people who are out of work, who live on council estates, or who have lived in Britain (or even at their present address) for a short time would find it difficult to obtain credit from a high street lender.

> *They won't give me a [bank] loan. I was going to get a loan to pay my bills. They said they had to get assurances from my credit card and I'm still owing, so they can't. I think what it is, they just look at the computer and they must see your name. And they just say 'No'.*

> *I went to see if [I could get a washing machine on HP at the fuel board]. I even had a hundred pound in my hand to pay down on it and then pay the rest off the [electricity] meter, and they wouldn't let me do it. You've got to pay it in cash or you've got to be working. Being on Income Support, it stops you getting credit.*

Some people anticipated that they would be refused credit by high street lenders and did not even bother to apply. Others, who had lost their jobs, had access to high street credit sources, such as overdrafts or credit cards, that they could have continued to use. But worries about running up unmanageable balances or the high charges for defaulting made them stop using them.

The only people who can afford to use credit cards are people who've got money in the first place. [If I continued to use it] I'd be even broker than I am today.

We were overdrawn on our overdraft by £2.19 and the bank charged us £59 and I wrote them a letter . . . and they apologised and said they would overlook it this time. It was crazy.

Moneylenders and doorstep traders offer a service that is quite distinct from high street lending and is geared to the needs of people living on low incomes. Instead of using statistical techniques to screen potential customers, they rely on personal recommendations from existing customers to attract new business.

We try to be very careful who we take on. We tend to only take on relatives of the people on the books, or friends. But if friends recommend it, the person recommending has to guarantee it to start off with.

They then use a much less formal method of assessing potential customers, taking into account personal as well as social and economic characteristics. These personal characteristics include honesty, trustworthiness and reliability. So, a young low-paid council tenant, who would find it difficult to get credit from a high street lender, might well obtain a loan from a moneylender. This would depend on what the moneylender knows, or can surmise, about their circumstances as well as their personality.

You look and you listen . . . say a young couple and there's not a lot in the house and they say they've got no credit, that I could believe. If they've got loads in the house, someone's telling you porkies . . . If it's, like today [very cold] and you go into someone's house and there's no heating on, you think 'Oh can they afford the heating?'

Having recruited a new customer, credit repayments are collected by the moneylender in person. Where possible, customers are visited on the day they are paid or receive their benefit cheque. By keeping tight control in this way, lenders can maximise their chances of being paid. Although this may seem heavy-handed, customers actually cited this as a positive advantage of moneylenders over credit cards or overdrafts.

The other main advantage to customers was that, although charges are high, they are fixed. If payments are missed there is no additional charge, unlike unpaid credit card bills or unauthorised overdrafts. This enabled people living on low incomes to retain control over their budgets and was one of the main reasons why some started using moneylenders, even though they still had access to other forms of revolving credit that they had acquired when they were more affluent.

Despite these advantages, there was little doubt that people incurred high costs if they used moneylenders (or for that matter pawnbrokers). Most loans were for relatively small sums of money for fairly short periods of time. And higher rates of interest were charged for shorter loans. In one company a 20-week loan incurred interest of 353 per cent APR, compared with 230 per cent APR for a 50-week loan.

Customers also maintained that they often felt under pressure to continue borrowing, sometimes against their better judgement. Some lenders used charm and cheek to get customers to borrow; others used higher pressure techniques.

As soon as the payments had finished, he got his wallet out and said, 'How much do you want?'

It's disgusting isn't it? But they always come round at the right time, when you need money, and you've got no choice. I mean it was Christmas, there was nothing I could do. It's too expensive and I wish I'd never started it . . .

(Kempson *et al*, 1994; Rowlingson, 1994; Speak *et al*, 1995.)

Financial exclusion

There is, however, a small section of the population that even licensed moneylenders are reluctant to take on as customers. Lone parents, pensioners, people living on certain high-rise estates and people who have bad payment records can all be excluded.

Lone parents who claimed Income Support were considered a bad risk because their budgets were usually stretched to the limit.

I'm not willing to take the chance [with lone parents], not now. I don't want to know that sort of business. When you first start, you tend to take a few more gambles.

Moneylenders were wary about people aged over 60, for fear that they might die, still owing the company a large sum of money. They were reluctant to take people over 60 on as new customers and actively tried to reduce the amount of money existing customers borrowed.

Fears for their own safety meant that moneylenders were not prepared to lend to people living on housing estates with a bad reputation. Contrary to their popular image, many moneylenders were women – especially those who worked for the largest national companies.

I wouldn't touch it with a barge pole. I used to when I started, but there's been muggings there. Plenty of women collectors have been mugged . . . there was a murder there a few weeks ago.

Then, there were people who were known to be bad payers. These were often put onto 'don't serve' (DS) lists and the information shared with other lenders in the neighbourhood, by marking the customer's door or door post. NBG that's the usual one – no bloody good!'

People who are denied loans from any licensed source of credit can be prey to loan sharks and unlicensed lenders. Most very poor housing estates have such lenders who are prepared to lend to almost anyone – at very high costs and with fairly draconian measures to ensure they are paid. On an inner city housing estate in Newcastle, many lone mothers knew of or had even used such lenders.

If I get short, I'll have to borrow, like . . . just a tenner one week and pay them back twenty next.

Twenty! That's a lot! I only give them £15 for a tenner. Mind, I don't know what it would be if I couldn't pay it back, like.

Cases were discussed openly of women who had given their benefit books to lenders, who met them outside the post office each benefit day to ensure the money was repaid.

In Oldham, unlicensed lenders took passports from people in the Bangladeshi population. There was also a fairly lucrative business for people who acted as 'go-betweens'. For a fee, they helped people who spoke little English, or who had been turned down, to gain access to credit.

(Kempson *et al*, 1994; Herbert and Kempson, 1996; Rowlingson, 1994; Speak *et al*, 1995.)

Over-commitment

While the wider availability of consumer credit may be welcome in some circumstances, it has undoubtedly added to the financial problems of many people, leading them into debt. Among low income families this was seldom due to straightforward overspending. More commonly it arose either where a drop in income left people with commitments they could no longer afford:

> *The reason we have been in financial difficulty is purely and simply because of the amount of money I earned. We could afford all these things and then, suddenly, within a month everything changes and you've no longer got that money.*

or where people had borrowed in an attempt to make ends meet or to pay other commitments:

> *When we owed them three payments [the moneylender] would come and, instead of saying 'do you want a loan', he'd get his wallet out and all you'd see was £10 and £20 notes and he'd say, 'Right, how much do you want?' . . . And they used to come constantly, they'd badger you into having money. We ended up owing them a fortune . . . They're the worst thing we were ever introduced to.*

Household utilities

Privatisation of the utilities began in 1984 with the sale of British Telecom, followed shortly afterwards by the sale of British Gas in 1986 and the water companies in 1989. The most recent privatisation was the electricity companies – in 1990.

The more commercial stance taken by companies, following privatisation, has raised a number of concerns regarding costs, payment facilities, debt recovery and universal access to services.

Charges

Much of the criticism levelled at the privatised utilities relates to their charges. Yet, there are some important differences between the utilities in how prices have changed since privatisation.

Both gas and electricity prices have fallen since privatisation, although the cost of electricity rose in the period immediately following the sale of the electricity companies. Since fuel bills account for a high proportion of low-income budgets, these price falls (before the imposition of VAT) were welcomed by low-income families.

In contrast, water charges have risen steeply since privatisation. In the five years following the sale of the water companies, average water bills increased by 67 per cent – many times the rate of inflation. As the charges rose, so did the risks of arrears. Research at the end of 1994 showed that people paying £5 a week or more had a high risk of default, especially if they had a low income. If they also had children, the risk of default was higher still. Almost four out of ten families with children, who paid over £5 a week and had incomes below £160 a week, were behind with their water bills.

Moreover, big variations in charges between water companies mean that low-income households in high-charge areas, like the South West, face greater hardship than other households in similar circumstances who live elsewhere.

Another significant change affecting low-income consumers is the separate billing of many council tenants, who used to have the charges included in their rent. This has meant another bill to be juggled and added to their risk of falling into arrears.

> At one time you paid everything with your rent, that was it so you didn't have to think about it. And then, of course, it all went private . . . I spent the last three years robbing Peter to pay Paul.

There are discussions within most of the utilities regarding the way that tariffs are distributed across customers. Until now there has been a degree of cross-subsidisation, which has generally favoured low-income consumers. But there are signs that this may be coming to an end. There has been a shift, with most utilities, towards increased standing charges accompanied by reductions in charges related to use. British Gas has reduced its tariff for people paying on direct debit on the grounds that their accounts are cheaper to administer. And the introduction of water metering has proved controversial, because it redistributes the tariff in such a way that it hits poor consumers who need to use large amounts of water, either for health reasons or because they have young children. Existing customers are not being forced to have water meters, but in some areas most new properties are being fitted with water meters automatically. Those who have a metered supply faced the familiar two choices: to go without or run the risk of being unable to pay the bill.

(Grant, 1995; Herbert and Kempson, 1995.)

Payment facilities

Paying utility bills is a constant headache for low-income households, especially where they have to be paid quarterly or half-yearly from a weekly income. Because more frequent payment methods are uneconomic for the supplier, they are not always advertised widely and tend to be available for people who think to ask or who have already fallen into arrears. Water company customer service representatives described the thinking behind this policy.

When we send reminders, we send out the little leaflet about people who are having payment problems. So anybody who gets these reminders and thinks, 'Oh God, I can't pay', we expect them to do something about it. And, if they ring up and say 'I can't pay this all at once', we would then offer them monthly or fortnightly and . . . the numbers who want frequent payments are manageable. Whereas, dare I say, if we advertised fortnightly or weekly payment booklets throughout, then the numbers would be much higher. So I am trying to . . . not exactly minimise, but target it.

The reason we don't advertise is because it is very costly for them and for us, if they are paying counter charges at a bank or post office.

In any case, where frequent payment options are available, the additional costs are often passed onto consumers. The same happens with pre-payment gas and electricity meters. Low-income consumers tend, as a result, to pay more for their fuel than customers who are better off.

Another trend across the utilities has been the encouragement of bill-payment by direct debit. Indeed, British Gas has gone further and introduced reduced tariffs for consumers paying their bills this way.

Direct debit arrangements were generally welcomed by people on low incomes who had bank accounts. But the fact remains that many low-income households did not have bank accounts or had chosen to stop using them. These tended to be the people who kept tighter control over their money and managed, more often than not, to pay their bills on time. Yet they did not receive any discount for prompt payment.

(Herbert and Kempson, 1995; Kempson *et al*, 1994; Morris and Ritchie, 1994; Speak *et al*, 1995.)

Debt recovery

Commercial pressures have made some utility companies adopt a fairly harsh approach to debt recovery, and rates of disconnection increased for telephones, gas and water following privatisation. More recently gas and water disconnections have fallen, but telephone disconnections remain high.

Yet the evidence suggests that arrears on fuel and water bills are largely concentrated among low-income households who *can't* rather than *won't* pay. Some utility companies have changed their debt recovery procedures to reflect this fact. Others retain an approach that is inappropriate to the circumstances of most of their customers in arrears.

Despite safeguards put into place at the time of privatisation, poor people, including many who have young children or are sick and disabled, are being disconnected from their telephone, fuel and water supplies. They then face a range of additional charges to get reconnected.

In 1994, water companies' reconnection fees ranged from £15 to £70. In some cases the customer also had to repay up to half of the arrears before they had their water reconnected. Finding this money caused great hardship. It was usually cobbled together by borrowing from family and friends and cutting back.

> *It was a lot of money to round up . . . We really didn't have enough to eat that week, because I'd paid them the £75. We lived on toast food really, there wasn't any substantial meals for the kids.*

People who had their telephone disconnected were also expected to pay a lump sum as a guarantee – even in cases of genuine hardship where the telephone was an essential service. For example, Brenda lived alone with her three-year-old daughter who had cerebral palsy and epilepsy and required constant care. When she received a very large telephone bill that she could not afford to pay, she asked for time to pay – explaining that she had needed to use the telephone on many occasions when her daughter required emergency medical treatment. Despite this she was disconnected.

Cecile had a number of chronic health problems and, having given up work, she could no longer afford to pay her telephone bill. She was disconnected and told she would have to repay her arrears before they would reconnect her telephone.

*I wrote to them asking, 'When I've finished paying this bill, what will happen?'
and they say I've got to pay £300 as a guarantee. £300! It's very hard and the
phone was so important because the girls can phone me up and see if I'm alright.*

(Grant, 1995; Herbert and Kempson, 1995; Kempson *et al*, 1994.)

Universal access
Such cases raise the question of universal access to the utilities, as they are
increasingly exposed to competition. In a competitive credit market, some
people are being denied access to any form of licensed credit. If a similar
situation were to occur with the essential utilities, the consequences would be
far more serious. It is not clear how the regulators would deal with this
situation.

Telephones are, so far, the only utility to have been opened up to competition,
although gas will soon follow suit. British Telecom has a very high rate of
disconnections (765,000 in 1994/5) and requires large guarantees for
reconnection. It has also introduced credit scoring to screen new applications for
telephones, which means some people being denied a telephone line. Since these
score cards will be very similar to those used in the high street credit industry,
we can expect the same groups of people to be excluded.

This exclusion was raised as a matter of concern in a study of teenage single
mothers. On one housing estate with a very high proportion of lone mothers,
only 26 per cent of the population had a telephone – compared with 92 per cent
nationally.

(Speak *et al*, 1995.)

Role of the regulators
At the time of privatisation, regulators were appointed for each of the main
utilities and a range of safeguards were written into licences to protect
consumers.

Regulators do, however, have limited terms of reference. They do not have the
power to legislate and have to balance potentially conflicting interests –
ensuring that the utility companies receive a reasonable rate of return, as well as
protecting the interests of consumers. In some cases they are also concerned
with ensuring competition. Individual regulators differ in the ways that they
interpret these responsibilities.

A study of water debt concluded that there were wide variations in the ways that water companies conducted their business and that Ofwat should play more of role in protecting consumers:

> ... *ensuring that water remains affordable for low-income customers, that they are offered payment options that ease budgeting problems and are treated equitably when they get into arrears.*

It also concluded that many of the safeguards to protect people from disconnection when they were in financial hardship were not doing so in reality.

(Herbert and Kempson, 1995.)

Summary

Deregulation of the credit industry has widened the availability of relatively low-cost commercial credit to people with modest incomes. It has, however, done little for the very poorest people, who have to use expensive sources of commercial credit, such as moneylenders and pawnbrokers. There are some low-income groups – lone parents, pensioners and people living on housing estates with bad reputations – who may not have access to any form of licensed credit. The only people prepared to lend to them are unlicensed 'loan sharks'.

The wider availability of credit has helped many people who live on a low income to spread the costs of household goods and equipment and to cope with peaks and troughs in their income and expenditure. But it has carried a price. Credit commitments taken out when people had an earned income soon became liabilities when their incomes dropped. And people who lived on low incomes and relied on commercial credit for bill-paying and making ends meet soon got into financial difficulties.

Privatisation of the utilities has not always benefited low-income consumers. The price of gas and electricity may have dropped slightly (discounting the effect of VAT), but water charges have risen appreciably. Moreover, the more commercial approach being taken by some utility companies to bill-payment facilities and debt recovery has hit low-income consumers the hardest. And there are concerns about poor people retaining access to essential services, as the utilities are opened up to competition.

7 Social security and fiscal policy

Social security and fiscal policy are central to the living standards of people on low incomes, and important changes in each of these areas have contributed to the increase in income inequalities over the past decade.

Most people living on low incomes rely on social security benefits to some degree, whether as their main source of income or to top up low wages. As a consequence, the wide-ranging changes in both social security policy and practice have had a major impact on their lives. Since the early 1980s benefit levels have, generally, been linked to prices, so that claimant incomes have failed to keep pace with those of the rest of the population. The late 1980s saw substantial reforms of the social security system – particularly of means-tested benefits. The aims of these reforms were to simplify the system, control spending and target payments on specific groups. And in many of these changes there is an emphasis on the use of discretion in determining entitlement. There have also been significant changes to the way that benefits are administered which, although they were designed to simplify claiming and reduce costs, have often had an unintended impact on the budgets of claimants.

Fiscal changes

Since many poor people pay little or no direct taxes, it might be thought that fiscal changes would affect their lives very little. But the shift from direct to indirect taxation has meant that people living on low incomes now carry a higher tax burden than they did 10 or 15 years ago. And the reforms of local taxation have, in many cases, added to that burden. Both these changes have had a disproportionate effect on people whose incomes have risen least over that period – people on fixed, low incomes and those dependent on social security for their income.

Shift towards indirect taxation
Successive budgets have brought about a continuing shift from direct to indirect taxation. As a consequence, people with low and middle incomes have borne the brunt of fiscal change. Direct taxation, through income tax, has the effect of slowing down income inequalities, since it takes a bigger proportion of higher than of lower incomes. In contrast indirect taxation, such as VAT, generally has a greater impact on people with low incomes and has the effect of increasing

inequalities. Yet the past 15 years have seen a reduction in the proportion of taxation collected in income tax and an increase in the amount raised through National Insurance contributions and indirect taxes such as VAT (Joseph Rowntree Foundation, 1995).

The effects of tax shifts of this kind are easier to demonstrate in quantitative research studies than in those adopting a qualitative approach. When discussing their household budgets, people seldom point to tax changes as having improved their financial position or made it worse. The exceptions are where tax has been changed on a single good – customs excise on cigarettes and VAT on fuel, for example.

Part of the rationale offered for increasing excise duty on tobacco is the hope that increasing the price of cigarettes will encourage people to give up smoking. Increases have, however, hit poor people more than those who are more affluent. As already seen in Chapter 1, people on low incomes are more likely to smoke than those who are better off, with many saying they would smoke less if they had fewer financial worries. As cigarette prices went up, the strain on their budget increased to the point that many women smokers reported going without food.

Likewise, the introduction of VAT (at 8 per cent) on fuel has affected people living on a low income. As we have seen, people living on Income Support often face a dilemma – to cut back fuel use or delay paying the bills. The increase in prices resulting from the imposition of VAT has only served to heighten that dilemma.

(Dobson *et al*, 1994; Dowler and Calvert ,1995; Herbert and Kempson, 1995; Kempson *et al*, 1994; Morris and Ritchie, 1994; Speak *et al*, 1995.)

Local taxes
Revisions of local taxation (the Poll Tax or Community Charge in particular) have increased the levels of payments made by many low-income households, especially those containing two or more adults. Pensioners, many of whom gained from the introduction of the Poll Tax, subsequently faced higher bills when it was replaced by the Council Tax.

The effects of these changes were amplified by the way that they were handled by the benefit system. From April 1988 until April 1993 the maximum rebate for local taxes was 80 per cent, so that Income Support claimants, as well as others on means-tested benefits, were expected to make up the difference from their general income. Income Support payments were increased to cover this extra outlay, but, in practice, the amount that claimants received was often insufficient to cover the amount they actually had to pay. Poor people tended to live in areas where charges were high, yet the extra benefit was based on a notional average charge. Full rebates were restored when the Council Tax was introduced.

Without doubt, the introduction of the Poll Tax, together with the requirement that people on Income Support had to pay 20 per cent of the charge, had a major effect on the budgets of people living on a low income. Previously their rates had been met in full if they were on Income Support, and those in low-paid employment paid their rates with their rent. These changes caused significant problems for low-income households, who simultaneously faced an increase in their outgoings and an additional payment to be made.

> *It wasn't refusing to pay it. It was just that we had to pay it out of our food money . . . Even if we were paying a fiver a week, we had to pay that fiver from food money.*

Many defaulted on their Poll Tax charges and were taken to court for non-payment. In one study more than half of 74 families with children, who were claiming either Income Support or Family Credit, had fallen into arrears with their Poll Tax and it was the single most common source of debt. Two years after the Poll Tax was replaced by Council Tax many still had outstanding debts. Indeed, many still do. Fewer people on low incomes now report major problems paying their Council Tax, although the 'can't pay, won't pay' attitude that the Poll Tax engendered has spilt over to some extent.

(Grant, 1995; Herbert and Kempson, 1995; Kempson *et al*, 1994; Morris and Ritchie, 1994.)

Benefit levels

From the early 1980s, levels of key social security benefits (including Income Support and the state pension) have been uprated in line with prices; whereas, previously, they were linked with rises in either prices or wages, whichever was the greater. And, since this decision was taken, prices have consistently grown more slowly than wage levels. People who had lived on benefits for some time often commented that they had found it progressively harder to manage on the money they received. A lone mother who had lived on Income Support for a number of years summed up the situation of many in her position.

There's not enough money to pay what you've got to pay . . . it seems like I'm in a poverty trap . . . every year it seems to get worse.

In explaining why he was in arrears with his water bill, a 75-year-old pensioner replied 'Cos my little bit of pension does not go up every six months or so'. If the link with wages had been retained, then a single person's basic state pension would now be £19 more than the £58.85 he would be receiving. A pensioner couple would receive £30 on top of the current £94.10 payments.

The situation with Child Benefit is less straightforward. Over the period from 1985 to 1990 there has been a reduction in its real value, but it is maintained, by the government, that families claiming either Income Support or Family Credit were cushioned from the effects of these cuts. The 1988 social security reforms sought to target assistance to low-income families by increasing the child premiums for these benefits.

It is difficult to judge the effects of these changes from qualitative research. What is clear, however, is the extent to which many mothers living on low incomes rely on their Child Benefit payments to meet everyday living expenses.

They give you enough to survive on. We get our money on a Monday, and we save the family allowance until the end of the week, so we've got enough for the weekend, for a Sunday meal, otherwise we wouldn't survive on the bit we get.

I draw my Income Support each week to live on and then I use the other [Child Benefit] to pay the bills . . . I don't have any money to put away for bills so I use that for bills.

(Dobson *et al*, 1994; Herbert and Kempson, 1995; Kempson *et al*, 1994; Middleton *et al*, 1995; Morris and Ritchie 1994; Speak *et al*, 1995.)

Social security reform

The Social Security Act 1986 brought about changes to means-tested benefits from April 1988, which were designed to produce a simplified and more harmonised system and have had far reaching effects.

• Income Support replaced Supplementary Benefit.

• The Social Fund replaced single payments for Income Support claimants with one-off needs.

- Family Credit replaced Family Income Supplement for low-waged families with dependent children.

- All the main means-tested benefits, including Housing Benefit, were simplified and aligned with Income Support.

In addition, the Act changed provisions of the State Earnings Related Pension Scheme (SERPS) and Widows Benefits.

Since the 1986 Act there have been further social security reforms, which included the benefits payable to sick and disabled people.

Income Support

The changes involved in the replacement of Supplementary Benefit by Income Support were complex. Additional weekly payments for special needs and other extra payments (for example for householders and people who had been on benefit long-term) were replaced by age-related allowances and premia for certain broad claimant groups. Single payments were separated from the system of weekly benefit and the Social Fund established in their place (see below) and there were a range of other changes designed to simplify the system. These included requiring claimants to pay 20 per cent of their local taxes and water rates from weekly benefit and ending the provisions for deducting work expenses (including childcare) from earnings when calculating entitlement to Income Support (see below). Finally some groups, such as students and most 16–17 year olds, lost entitlement to benefit altogether.

Because these changes were so wide ranging it has proved difficult to estimate the effects on particular groups of claimants. A study undertaken for the *Inquiry into Income and Wealth* concluded that, as intended, families with children gained overall. But they had no guarantee against losing and, comparing the situations in 1987/8 and 1990/1, about a half of single parents and a third of couples with children had less money under the new scheme. Other groups who gained overall included pensioners and people who were sick or disabled; while unemployed people without children generally received less assistance. But, again, the situations were not straightforward and there were winners and losers in each of these groups (Evans, 1994; Evans *et al*, 1994).

Low-income families with children, nevertheless, have a very high risk of financial problems and arrears – suggesting that benefit rates are not high enough. It is also because, as we have seen, parents try to protect their children from the effects of poverty. In one study there was little difference between what parents on Income Support considered a minimum essential budget for their children and the amount agreed by parents with close to average incomes. And, depending on the age of the child, these were between £6 and £13 a week more than the Income Support child allowance and family premium in 1994.

Younger unemployed people without children have, meanwhile, seen an increase in their risk of financial problems following the social security reforms. A recent study of water debt found that single people had as high a risk of arrears as families with children (Herbert and Kempson, 1995).

Stuart, for example, was in arrears with his water charges and still owed money in unpaid Poll Tax. Both were being deducted at source from his Income Support payments. As a result he received £78 a fortnight. This had to cover all his living expenses except his rent, which was met in full. When he collected his benefit cheque he immediately bought £15 of tokens for his electricity meter and paid £5 towards a court fine. He had come to rely on a mail-order catalogue for clothes and presents for his family and his payments on that were £25 a fortnight. His telephone bill was, on average, £10 a fortnight, while his gas bills had been unpaid for nearly a year. This left him just over £20 a fortnight for food and other housekeeping, as well as the bus fares and postage he incurred when looking for work.

The group hit hardest by the reforms, however, is young people. Most of those aged 16 and 17 lost their entitlement to benefit altogether, and single people and childless couples between the ages of 18 and 24 received a reduced level of benefit. This reduction was based on the assumption that they would be living at home with their parents and a government guarantee that 16 and 17 year olds would be in a youth training scheme. In practice many are not.

Consequently, young people who are unable to continue living at home face very real financial difficulties, especially if their parents offer them no support. For example, Charlie had left home at 15, following his father's remarriage and arguments with his new stepmother. At the time of the 1988 social security changes he was unemployed, his benefit was stopped and he had to take a place on a youth training scheme. He received £30 for working a full week, out of which he was expected to pay £11.50 a week deductions for rent, Poll Tax and electricity arrears.

I went up to see them about that and they says there was nothing they could do about it.

In another study of single homeless people, housing managers commented on the difficulties faced by 16 and 17 year olds when they were offered permanent accommodation.

I don't know how 16 and 17 year olds survive anyway if they're given a tenancy, because of the amount of money they've actually got to live on . . . I mean who could budget on that sort of income? It's ludicrous.

Young pregnant women faced similar problems. Pregnancy does not make a young woman incapable of work, although in practice research has shown that many had difficulties finding an employer who was willing to offer them a youth training place. Even so, they did not qualify for Income Support until 11 weeks before the confinement, when (in 1994) 16 and 17 year olds received about £35 a week if they did not live with their parents; 18 year olds got £44.

(Bines, 1994; Herbert and Kempson, 1995; Jones, 1995; Middleton *et al*, 1994; Speak *et al*, 1995.)

Social Fund

The Social Fund is the latest in a series of measures which have been designed to help people on basic means-tested benefit meet one-off needs. But unlike its predecessors (exceptional needs payments from 1948 to 1980 and single payments from 1980 to 1988) the Social Fund is a separate scheme that is cash limited and, in many cases, provides loans rather than grants. It has drawn a great deal of criticism on both these counts.

In fact there are a number of components to the Social Fund. First, there are mandatory payments for maternity and funeral expenses and during very cold weather. Then there is a discretionary fund offering a mix of loans and grants:

- budgeting loans: repayable by direct deductions from benefit, to enable Income Support claimants to meet immediate lump sum needs

- crisis loans: to meet urgent needs, often for living expenses, which are available to a wider group of claimants

- community care grants: for people moving out of institutions to live in the community or to help them remain in the community; and for families who are 'under exceptional pressure'. These grants are only available to people on Income Support, or who are about to claim it.

In practice, there is a much higher refusal rate for grants and the majority of successful applicants receive a loan.

There have, however, been well-documented difficulties with the Fund. These principally relate to the lack of grants, to applications being turned down due to cash limits on the Fund, and to the relatively high repayments that are deducted at source from benefit.

Many people were angry that they were expected to take a loan, especially when they needed money because benefit levels were inadequate to meet essentials.

> *I don't think that you should have to pay for necessities . . . I think that loans for most people on social security are a complete farce.*

> *It's silly because you borrowed it in the first place because you was short.*

> *I still reckon some things they ought to give you the money for, a grant . . . There is some people who genuinely need more than the Social let them have.*

Cash-limiting, allied with discretion, meant that decisions made by Social Fund Officers often seemed arbitrary, with people in similar circumstances being treated differently.

> *I've got a friend who applied three times for the Social Fund. She was accepted three times. Someone else didn't get accepted at all.*

> *Basically I wanted £145 for a cooker. They refused it, said they didn't have the funds. That very afternoon a lad that lived down that way went in for exactly the same thing for the same reasons and they gave it to him.*

In other cases people were offered less than they needed, or restrictions were placed on the purposes for which loans were given. Many applicants had become wise to the criteria applied by their local office and lied in order to get what they needed.

> *They always knock you down. So you always ask for that little bit more, knowing that they'll knock you down.*

> *You have to tell all the lies you can to get the Social Fund. Telling the truth you don't get anything . . . No-one ever gets what they want.*

A worrying trend is the rise in refusals because applicants are considered too poor to pay back a loan. Figures released by the Benefits Agency to MP Alan Milburn show they doubled from 44,890 in 1992/3 to 116,095 in 1993/4. A teenage mother in financial difficulties, for example, wanted to apply for a grant.

They said I'd not get a grant, so I didn't waste my time asking, just went for a loan. Then if they didn't go and tell me I couldn't afford to pay it back so I couldn't have one. Well that's why I wanted a grant, isn't it? Stupid!

The other main difficulty with the Fund is the high repayments people were expected to make. Compared with most commercial credit, Social Fund loans were repayable over a shorter period of time. This meant that weekly payments were often £5 or more a week, which placed a further strain on finances that were usually overstretched to begin with.

Having to pay back so much is helping to get us into trouble. We don't have any choice about paying this, we can't leave it one week to pay for something else . . . they take it straight out of your dole.

Even so, the Social Fund was generally much preferred to using commercial credit. Most who used it had only limited access to commercial credit and this tended to be restricted to the most expensive sources, such as moneylenders and pawnbrokers. They were attracted to using the Social Fund because loans were interest-free and repayments were deducted at source from their benefit. Moreover, they felt that they were less likely to become over-committed because Social Fund Officers had a better understanding of the financial circumstances of claimants than did commercial creditors.

At least with [the Social Fund] they work out what you can afford to pay them back . . . Whereas if you get into debt with [commercial creditors] they don't care . . . You hear about so many things, that they'll take things away and come into your house.

(Grant, 1995; Kempson *et al*, 1994; Morris and Ritchie, 1994; Speak *et al*, 1995.)

Work expenses and childcare costs

Changes from 1988 onwards meant that work expenses could no longer be offset against earnings by those claiming Income Support. Such costs have to be met out of the small amount of earnings claimants are allowed to retain (£15 for a lone mother; £5 for most others). This potentially affected most groups of

Income Support claimants to some extent. But the effects were greatest for lone parents who could no longer set the costs of childcare against any money they earned.

However, since October 1994, a childcare disregard of £40 a week was introduced for mothers working more than 16 hours a week and who are, therefore, eligible for Family Credit. But the initial evidence suggests that the new disregard has had little real impact. Few lone mothers knew about it and most had difficulty understanding how it worked and whether it would help them. Moreover, it has been concluded that few mothers would be able to go to work as a direct result of the new childcare disregard, because it is not sufficient to cover even one child receiving full-time care. In the November 1995 budget it was announced that the disregard would be increased to £60, which might well increase its impact.

(Kempson et al, 1994; Speak et al, 1995; Third, 1995.)

Family Credit
Compared with Family Income Supplement, Family Credit was more generous and covered a larger number of families. However, other factors such as the loss of free school meals and the fact that Family Credit reduced Housing Benefit entitlement meant that the new benefit was not always as generous as it seemed (Evans, 1994; Evans et al, 1994).

There can be little doubt that, in the current job market, families with children have benefited from the introduction of Family Credit. The research shows that, compared with similar families claiming Income Support, those receiving Family Credit have fewer financial problems. They are less likely to face the dilemma of going without essentials or falling into arrears. Consequently they are much less likely to be in debt and, where they are, their arrears tend to be for smaller sums and to a smaller number of creditors.

Lone mothers, in particular, have been helped by Family Credit, since it has enabled them to take part-time jobs to fit in with childcare but, with benefit, receive a full-time wage for doing so. When Family Credit was first introduced, it was necessary to work 24 hours a week to claim. This was later reduced to 16 hours in 1992, enabling more families (especially lone parents) to move off Income Support and increase their incomes.

Although this change helped families with children it has adversely affected those without, especially if they were home owners. It meant that those working between 16 and 24 hours a week lost entitlement to Income Support and the associated mortgage interest assistance and (because there is no 'mortgage benefit' equivalent to Housing Benefit) had to meet their mortgage payments in full. Many were worse off as a consequence.

(Kempson *et al*, 1994; Morris and Ritchie, 1994.)

Sickness and disability benefits

Benefits for sick and disabled people were not revised in the 1986 Act and awaited the results of a major study of disabled people's circumstances being undertaken by OPCS. Since then, three new benefits have been introduced: Disability Working Allowance, Disability Living Allowance and Incapacity Benefit.

Disability Working Allowance (DWA) is a means-tested benefit, similar to Family Credit, which tops up incomes for low-waged people with disabilities – including those without children . There is, however, little evidence to suggest that DWA has had the same impact assisting disabled people into work as Family Credit seems to have had with parents. This is largely because the barrier to work is not so much a financial one, but (as we have seen in Chapter 4) that employers are unwilling to recruit people with health problems.

Disability Living Allowance (DLA) is a non-means-tested additional benefit paid to disabled people aged under 65 who have either a severe mobility impairment or need supervision or personal care. It, therefore, replaced Mobility Allowance and Attendance Allowance for such people. Those aged over 65 who need care can still apply for Attendance Allowance, but there is no benefit provision for people who acquire a severe mobility impairment after the age of 65.

The level of DLA varies with the severity of the impairment but, since it is disregarded when entitlement to means-tested benefits is calculated, can add significantly to people's incomes from Income Support.

Those who had applied successfully frequently commented on the difference it had made to their finances – although it was often used to pay general household bills rather than to meet the costs of special needs.

> *Well, normally, when I get my monthly money [DLA] I have got to pay all my big things out, like my gas . . . So all my big bills I leave them until my monthly money's due.*

If disabled people have to use the DLA for day-to-day living costs in this way, then the extent to which it meets the intended needs is a matter of debate.

Moreover, DLA has eligibility rules which mean that some people are unable to claim at all even when they incur additional costs as a result of their impairment. People who do not qualify include those with epilepsy, with chronic asthma, with mental health problems, with chronic heart conditions and those with some visual or hearing impairments.

Colin, for example, was profoundly deaf and occasionally employed an interpreter to improve the quality of his life. He had applied for DLA but had been turned down. So he met the costs, when he could, out of his Income Support payments of £44 a week.

Charlotte had ME and was frequently unable to walk, cook her own meals or even reach the bathroom without help. Even though there were spells when she needed constant care and support, she, too, had her application for DLA turned down.

The most recent change to sickness and disability benefits is the introduction of *Incapacity Benefit*, in April 1995, to replace Invalidity and Sickness Benefits. It is too early for the results of research looking at the impact of the new benefit. There is, however, some evidence that people who had been claiming Invalidity Benefit were not being transferred to Incapacity Benefit, although they were still considered unfit for work by employers and Jobcentres.

This had happened to a young man with severe learning difficulties, who was cared for by his mother. He was judged fit for work and, in transferring from Invalidity Benefit to Income Support as an unemployed person, he lost £20 a week. Yet the Disability Resettlement Officer told him that he had almost no chance of finding work as they lived in an area of very high unemployment.

In another case, a man was transferred off Invalidity Benefit which he had claimed since an accident at work. He questioned this decision, not just because he felt that he was not fit enough to work, but because of the inadequacy of the medical examination that had informed the decision.

> *The doctor I saw, he didn't have all my files there so how can he assess you if he hasn't got all your files. He didn't ask me anything. He just said 'Strip off round there, lift your foot'. He checked my reflexes and that were basically it. They haven't even found my X-rays from when I had the accident. That's what I can't get over.*

He, too, lost £20 a week, which was a major reason for him falling into debt. Detailed research is needed to assess whether these are exceptional cases or part of a larger problem.

(Grant, 1995; Rowlingson, 1994.)

Child Support Agency

The Child Support Agency was set up in 1993 to recover maintenance from absent parents. And, although the Agency is not part of the social security system, rising social security expenditure on lone parents was an important driving force for its establishment.

From the outset, the Agency was the subject of controversy, with the most vociferous criticism coming from better-off absent fathers who claimed that the levels of maintenance fixed by the Agency were too high and that it had targeted fathers who were already contributing towards their children's upkeep. The views of mothers, however, were given rather less publicity by the media.

When the Agency was first proposed, many lone mothers expressed strong support for the principle underlying the Child Support Act, believing that it was only right that absent fathers should pay towards the keep of their children where they could.

> *Oh aye, it's a good thing, I suppose. Well why shouldn't they have to pay out for them. It's not just the mother's responsibility. And it makes you feel bad knowing that you have to live on Social all the time.*

Two years after the Agency was set up, most lone mothers still supported the general principle (especially when the decision to have the child had been a joint decision), but were rather more equivocal as a result of their experiences. Long delays in assessments (often a year or more) were commonplace and accompanied by a lack of information or incorrect information from the Child Support Agency.

> *Sometimes I feel like getting on the phone . . . to find out why they got me to fill out all those forms in the first place and then they've done nothing about it.*

Few mothers felt they were any better off financially. Indeed, those claiming Income Support lose benefit pound for pound and any maintenance paid goes to the Treasury, not to lone parent families.

It's fair what he's supposed to pay, just not bloody fair that we don't get it. It's really awful, just for the Government and Treasury, not for families. 'The party of the family' – it's a joke!

Potentially, lone mothers who work should be better off, although those claiming Family Credit gain only £15 a week, anything more than this reduces their benefit entitlement. In practice, though, few working lone mothers said they were any better off. Even where assessments had been processed, maintenance payments were often unreliable, leaving mothers on Family Credit short of money in the weeks their maintenance was not paid.

Moreover, many mothers lost informal help from their children's fathers if the Child Support Agency assessment was for more maintenance than they had previously paid.

He used to buy them a lot of clothes and take them on holiday, but that's all cut down now . . . he's struggling to give them much at all.

When the mother worked, this generally cancelled out the extra money she received in maintenance. If she claimed Income Support she was often worse off.

Many mothers (like the vociferous fathers) were angry that the Child Support Agency had targeted absent fathers who were already paying some maintenance and had not pursued those who were not. This view was held both by women whose partners did not pay and those who already had maintenance agreements.

. . . they are picking on the wrong ones for a start . . . it's the ones that are paying maintenance that are getting chased up.

It's the people who are not paying they should be contacting . . . I think they should leave people in my situation alone.

This targeting seems to have stemmed from the need to achieve substantial savings in social security expenditure. Since these interviews were carried out, however, such targets have largely been replaced by ones to improve the speed and accuracy of maintenance assessments (Child Support Agency, 1995).

Intervention by the Child Support Agency also increased friction between ex-partners and often coloured women's support for the principle underlying its work.

I believe in the CSA in theory, but in practice it is a totally different thing. I do believe the father should support the children, but in practice the way they are going about it, it is a nightmare.

(Clarke *et al*, 1996; Kempson *et al*, 1994; Speak *et al*, 1995.)

Benefit administration

Besides the introduction of new benefits, there have been substantial changes to the way that benefits are administered. Housing Benefit administration was transferred to local authorities. Payment of Statutory Sick Pay and Maternity Pay were transferred to employers. And, as part of the Next Steps initiative, a range of agencies has been set up to administer various aspects of the social security system at 'arm's length' from the Department of Social Security.

The most important of these agencies, for benefit claimants, was the Benefits Agency, with its network of local offices. Since it was set up in April 1991, the Benefits Agency has made great efforts to improve the way that it administers the assessment and payment of benefit. It is generally recognised as having achieved a good deal, but problems still remain – largely because of the complexity of the benefits system.

Introduction of changes

Many changes to the social security system have been introduced rapidly and some were far from smooth. Problems with the Child Support Agency have attracted a great deal of attention and have been described in some detail above. But other changes have also caused problems for claimants.

The administration of Housing Benefit was transferred to local authorities before many of them had the necessary computer systems in place. This led to delays and errors in benefit payments, causing many claimants to fall into debt.

The introduction of the Disability Living Allowance was also problematic for applicants, who faced long delays before the outcome of their claims were determined.

Errors and delays

Aside from the introduction of new benefits, advice workers report that the frequency of errors and delays in benefit payment have been reduced. But, where they occur, they still cause hardship to the claimants affected. A study of elderly stroke victims, who were returning to live in the community, found that delays in the assessment of benefit made it difficult for them to play an active role in planning their own care. In other instances, delays to housing benefit claims had led to arrears and acted as a disincentive to people taking low-paid work that they felt might be insecure.

(Baldock and Ungerson, 1994; Ford *et al*, forthcoming.)

Changes in circumstance

One area that frequently gave rise to difficulties was the need for claimants to notify changes in their circumstances. Many failed to realise they were required to do this, which led to both overpayment and underpayment of benefit and a disruption to household budgets. A particular difficulty arose from the separate administration of Housing Benefit by local authorities. Many claimants assumed that if the Benefits Agency knew about their change in circumstance, there was no need to tell the local authority too. They expected the relevant information to be transferred automatically.

Harry, for example, had not informed his local authority when he became eligible for Invalidity Benefit rather than Sick Pay.

My money changed to Invalidity . . . but I carried on paying same rent. I got a minimum rent rise that coincided with getting Invalidity, so I thought they'd adjusted my rent.

The error meant that he accumulated £450 of rent arrears, which he was struggling to repay out of a weekly income of £113 for himself and his wife.

(Ford *et al*, forthcoming; Grant, 1995; Kempson *et al*, 1994.)

Frequency of benefit payment

There have been some important changes to the way that benefits are paid. While most people who live on a low income tend to budget weekly, many benefits are paid fortnightly, with Child Benefit paid monthly.

Fortnightly payments made the task of budgeting even more difficult, especially for those who were inclined to a pay-as-you-go approach. In such circumstances they needed to take extra steps to make sure that they did not run short before the end of the fortnight. Chapter 1 has shown how women tended to adopt a fortnightly shopping pattern to fit in with benefit receipt. Some also put money into savings accounts so that they would not be tempted to spend the next week's housekeeping. In contrast, monthly Child Benefit was often welcomed by mothers as it presented a way of putting some money aside to meet their children's needs.

Not only was the frequency of payment changed but, in addition, Income Support is now paid in arrears. This often causes hardship to new claimants and is one of the main reasons for applications for crisis loans for day-to-day living expenses from the Social Fund.

(Kempson *et al*, 1994; Middleton *et al*, 1994.)

Direct payments from benefit

The number of direct payments from Income Support has grown considerably, with water payments alone increasing from 55,000 in May 1991 to 216,000 in February 1994. Most direct payments are for arrears (on water, gas, electricity, rent, mortgage or Council and Poll Tax). Benefit overpayments, Social Fund loans, fines and maintenance payments can also be deducted at source. And almost all assistance with housing costs is now paid direct to the landlord or mortgage lender. The rules governing direct payments are complex. There is a maximum amount that can be deducted at source, but this can be exceeded if the claimant agrees.

Direct payments undoubtedly caused hardship even if they were sometimes welcomed as a way of getting straight financially. There were cases where people were losing a large proportion of benefit at source – like Charlie, above, who was paying £11.50 out of his £30 a week benefit. In fact, direct payments were identified as one of the main reasons why some people on Income Support failed to make ends meet.

Problems were also faced when people stopped claiming Income Support and lost the facility to have arrears paid direct. They then needed to renegotiate with their creditors, who were not always as sympathetic when they were in work.

(Herbert and Kempson, 1995; Kempson *et al*, 1994; Jones, 1995; Speak *et al*, 1995.)

Information and advice

The Benefits Agency has made great efforts to improve the quality of its information and advice service, but, despite aspirations to provide a 'one-stop shop', claimants still find this aspect of the service wanting. The most common complaint is that people are given general information rather than advice related to their specific needs.

Before giving up her job to care for her disabled husband, Kate had visited her local Benefits Agency office to discuss the benefits they would be entitled to claim.

In December . . . We went and spoke to social security before I finished and they worked out everything that we should get . . . And they told us not to worry everything would be taken care of. We would get X amount of pounds, plus they would pay the mortgage . . . It got to March and I suddenly got a court summons because we were in arrears with our mortgage . . . because, unknown to us, nobody had explained that, for the first so many weeks, you have to pay so much . . . Well, I mean, it was devastating, we nearly lost the house. I ended up owing £2,000 which, I mean, it was terrifying. Why didn't social security say to us 'there is so much left that you have to pay'?

This was far from an isolated incident. A number of other home buyers on Income Support had been confused about their mortgage payments.

We have already seen (Chapter 5) that private tenants were unable to get advice about the level of Housing Benefit they could expect to receive on properties they were considering renting. Moreover, lack of information about in-work benefits was a major disincentive to some people taking low-paid work. And even when they asked for advice, it was often not provided.

(Ford *et al*, forthcoming; Grant, 1995; Kempson *et al*, 1994; Law *et al*, 1994.)

Benefit take-up

Perhaps the most important consequence of inadequate information is the failure of some people to claim the benefits to which they are entitled. As Table 8 shows, substantial numbers of households do not claim benefits to which they are entitled. Moreover, the sums of money involved (more than £20 a week for Housing Benefit, Income Support and Family Credit) are such that they could make a substantial difference to people's ability to make ends meet.

Lone parents, other families with children and local authority tenants tend to have the highest take-up rates. Take-up is lowest among pensioners, non-pensioner households without children and home owners.

The research suggests that information is needed to alert people to benefits for which they might be eligible and also to combat their reluctance to claim.

Table 8 Non-take-up of benefit

Benefit	Range of non-take-up (%)	Range of entitled non-recipients (000)	Average weekly amount unclaimed (£)
Housing Benefit	4–12	200–600	21.45
Council Tax Benefit	20–29	1340–2170	5.45
Family Credit	29	180	24.00
Income Support	12–21	720–1390	22.85

Source: Department of Social Security, *Income related benefit: estimates of take-up in 1993/4.* DSS, 1995.

Lack of knowledge

Without a doubt, means-tested in-work benefits are the main area where lack of knowledge leads to people not applying for benefits they are entitled to claim.

Few tenants who were out of work had a clear idea of whether they would get any Housing Benefit if they took a low-paid job. Hardly any knew in detail how much Housing Benefit they would be likely to get and they were outnumbered by those who assumed that, if they took a job, they would get no help with their rent at all. When asked how much Housing Benefit they thought they might receive on their minimum acceptable wage, the great majority underestimated the amount.

Department of Social Security statistics show that in 1993/4 between 200,000 and 610,000 households were not claiming Housing Benefit to which they were entitled. The average amount unclaimed was £21.45 a week (see Table 8). Statistics are not available subdividing this into those claiming Income Support (and getting Housing Benefit automatically) and those who are not. It is, however, known that non-take-up is a great deal higher among those not on Income Support.

The effects of this are that many people fall into arrears not just with their rent, but with other bills too. Kazim, for example, had not claimed Housing Benefit at all and owed £1,500 in arrears. Barbara had not realised she needed to reapply when her Housing Benefit claim expired and, several months later, owed several hundred pounds in rent.

Family Credit has a relatively low rate of take-up. Despite national television advertising and notes in Child Benefit books, government statistics show that, in

1993/4, 29 per cent of eligible low-waged families (180,000 in total) were not claiming their entitlement. The average amount unclaimed was £24 a week (Department of Social Security, 1995). Again, there was clear confusion among potential claimants who were out of work.

There's Family Credit, but it wouldn't help me very much. It would probably only top me up to what I'm getting now.

They've got a thing on the family allowance book. But the thing is, I don't know how it works . . .

When asked how much Family Credit they thought they might get on their minimum acceptable wage, most people underestimated the amount. Most people who had not claimed, when they could have done, were entitled to relatively small sums. The aggravation of claiming had often put them off. But where the unclaimed amounts were more substantial, financial difficulties usually occurred.

The need to reapply for Family Credit every six months meant that some people failed to claim even though they were eligible. Cheryl was one of these. She was a care assistant in a residential home and had been receiving Family Credit until her claim ran out. She did not realise she needed to reapply and, as she had had a temporary promotion, assumed (wrongly) that she was no longer eligible and that was why her benefit payments had stopped. She had, consequently, fallen into arrears with bills.

The benefits available for sick and disabled people are very complex, being a mixture of contributory and means-tested benefits, with some benefits also involving medical criteria. It is little wonder that confusion arises about entitlement.

When Jerry became sick he received Statutory Sick Pay (which has no allowance for dependants), but had no other income to support him, his wife and their two small children. They had a total of £52.50 a week to live on and would almost certainly have been eligible for Income Support, Housing Benefit and Council Tax Benefit. During this time they had enormous difficulties making ends meet and ran up substantial arrears, which, according to his wife, they were still trying to pay off a year later.

Last year he took so many weeks off . . . but we never claimed anything while he was off sick. We never claimed anything off the Social. We didn't even know we were entitled to anything. He got normal statutory pay but we didn't claim anything else. So we were surviving off his bloody sick pay and then the bills weren't getting paid and everything was getting on top of us.

Tom had two adult children with learning difficulties, but for years he had not claimed any additional benefits on behalf of his children. The family had serious debt problems.

We knew nothing about claiming benefits for our children. We hadn't the faintest idea. I knew you could get certain things, but I thought they were for people who had epileptic fits or were paralysed. We didn't know it applied to people who were mentally handicapped as well as physically handicapped. We hadn't a clue. No-one told us anything. I was a bit peeved when I found out, after all this time. In actual fact it rather put me off social services because we had been in contact with them for many years.

Lack of knowledge was especially common among some ethnic minority groups. Chinese people, in particular, had little knowledge of benefits they might be eligible to claim. This was compounded because they knew neither where to get advice about entitlement nor where to apply for social security.

(Ford *et al*, forthcoming; Grant, 1995; Kempson *et al*, 1994; Law *et al*, 1994; Third, 1995.)

Reluctance to claim
Some people, who had been in work all their lives, were very resistant to the idea of claiming benefit when they lost their job. Jill and her husband Glenn, for example, had both been made redundant at about the same time and were eligible for Unemployment Benefit. But only Jill applied. Even though he had been out of work for three months, Glenn said 'I haven't bothered. I took it for granted that I'd get work by now.'

Self-employed people are particularly unlikely to claim benefit when they cease to trade. In part this is because of difficulties with social security rules. But it also arises from a reluctance to admit that their business has failed and that they are unemployed. Jim had been in this position and he and his wife lived on their savings and a £500 loan from their daughter until he found a job.

My husband wasn't working and he wasn't claiming. It was before I started work . . . I often wonder why I didn't have a nervous breakdown . . . It was my husband, his ideas like. He didn't want to claim, he thought it would get better.

As we have seen, there was also a resistance to claiming in-work benefits, with male breadwinners, in particular, feeling that if they took a job they wanted one that would lift them off benefits altogether.

Reluctance to claim was particularly common among devout Muslims. Some Bangladeshi and Pakistani people had been out of work for a year, but they had claimed no benefit at all. Claiming benefit while unemployed was felt to contradict the Islamic ethic of working for a living and earning your own money, and likely to bring *Sharam* (shame and embarrassment) on the whole family.

> *As a young person I don't want to go on the dole. I don't think people would approve of a young person being on benefit when I could find a job. This is why I have decided not to claim benefit yet. I wouldn't claim unless I had absolutely no money to buy necessities.*

> *As a Muslim I don't think it is right for me to go and claim while I am youthful and healthy. I should seek a job as long as I am able to survive without harming myself.*

In Islam, there is a principle that allows for concessions (such as claiming benefit) in cases of extreme hardship. But this only applies when all other possibilities, such as seeking support from family and friends, have been exhausted. Even then it can only be for a temporary period during which the person must feel guilt and be striving to improve their circumstances.

These beliefs about social security were strongest among young Muslims, who would most likely have claimed Income Support. The same was not necessarily so if men lost their jobs later in life. Here there was a strong feeling that claiming benefit was their *Haq* (right), having paid taxes and National Insurance all their lives.

(Ford *et al*, forthcoming; Grant, 1995; Kempson *et al*, 1994; Law *et al*, 1994; Third, 1995.)

Language problems

People with a limited or no ability to speak English faced very real difficulties in their dealings with the Benefits Agency. Interpreters were often provided by the agency, but had to be booked in advance, which delayed both the resolution of enquiries and the receipt of benefit. People overcame these difficulties by relying on relatives, or by seeking help from an advice agency, where this was available.

Women often felt that this discriminated against them, as their English was often poor and they had to rely on their male relatives. They felt this reinforced both patriarchal and dependent relationships and their general social isolation.

(Herbert and Kempson, 1996; Law *et al*, 1994.)

Current concerns

Three concerns tend to be uppermost in the debate about social security. First there is the rising cost of social security; with the emphasis on cutting expenditure, increasing work incentives and reducing levels of dependence on the state, and looking to private insurance provision. Closely linked to this is the concern about social security fraud. Finally there are concerns about the apparent failure of the social security system to respond to social and economic changes and the fact that it has had to pick up the costs of wider changes in social policy: changes in the labour market; shifts in housing tenure; the policy of care in the community; and the privatisation of utilities.

Rising costs

The costs of social security continue to rise, albeit more slowly, despite repeated attempts to curtail expenditure. In part, this has been a consequence of demographic changes – the growing numbers of elderly people and of lone parents, in particular. In part, it has arisen because the social security budget has been expected to pick up the costs of other areas of policy. High levels of unemployment and the changes in housing subsidies are the two most obvious examples (see Chapters 4 and 5).

Concerns about costs have led to a close scrutiny of criteria for entitlement, based on a belief that some people are claiming benefits they ought not to be receiving. Some of the recent policy changes that resulted have been already been discussed. They include the replacement of Invalidity Benefit by Incapacity Benefit, with stricter medical criteria for entitlement, and the imposition of rent restrictions on the Housing Benefit entitlement of tenants renting in the private sector.

The introduction of the Child Support Agency was also, in part, intended to reduce the amount spent on Income Support to lone mothers.

In addition, there have been two further shifts in policy designed to stem rising expenditure on social security. These are the requirement for unemployed people to demonstrate that they are actively looking for work and moves towards private insurance.

Proof of job search

Since 1989 unemployed people claiming benefit have had to be 'actively seeking work' and to produce proof that they are doing so, if required. This will be further tightened when the Jobseekers' Allowance comes into effect in 1996.

Yet there is little evidence to support the theory that unemployed people are content to remain dependent on the State and are refusing to take jobs. On the contrary, the qualitative research demonstrates clearly the lengths to which some people go to find work. Hence, the main effect of the requirements has been to encourage people to apply for jobs that they have no chance at all of getting, just to demonstrate that they are 'actively seeking work'.

Some spoke of 'going through the motions' of attending a job club and the futility of applying for a set number of jobs a week. Others referred to the disillusionment of constantly applying for jobs and not even getting an acknowledgement, still less an interview.

A 49-year-old man was desperate to find work and ashamed to be unemployed. Despite doing three Training for Work courses – in painting and decorating, carpentry and horticulture – he had been out of work for two years. He went to the Jobcentre four times a week, looked for work by going to factory gates, and answered advertisements in his local paper. In total he had applied for 109 jobs since becoming unemployed and felt that he had reached the end of the road. His experience was not that different from many others who had been out of work for a number of years.

Self-employed people are among those hit hardest by the rules. While they try to keep their businesses going they are considered not to be available for work and so are not eligible for benefit. For example, a man who had run a fleet of five lorries in the building trade had been hit by the recession. He had laid off all his drivers and sold four of the lorries. He waited by the telephone in the hope that work might come in and was considered ineligible for benefit.

There are also indications that staff at Jobcentres have been trying to persuade people to consider jobs that would give them less take-home pay than they feel they need to cover their outgoings. One study found that it was not uncommon for single unemployed men to be encouraged to lower their wage expectations. Two men had almost identical circumstances. Both had calculated that they needed about £150 a week if they were to cover all their bills, buy food and have about £20 a week for non-essentials or to put by for emergencies. In both cases they were told that unless they were prepared to consider jobs paying £120 a week they would lose Income Support payments. In a third case, a debt counsellor at a citizen's advice bureau had calculated that a divorced man would need to earn £150 a week to cover his outgoings, including the increased maintenance he would be required to pay to his ex-wife. When he visited the Jobcentre it was suggested that he could live on £25–35 less, without any real consideration of his needs.

(Ford *et al*, forthcoming.)

Moves towards private insurance and pensions
Rising social security bills have raised the prospect that private insurance and pensions might play a greater role in providing financial assistance following job loss, sickness and retirement. This, in turn, raises the possibility of a further widening of inequalities as those in better-paid, secure jobs will be in the best position to make private provision.

The effects of this can already be seen among pensioners. Those with occupational pensions are appreciably better off than people drawing just the state pension. Research shows that pensioners living on only the state pension often struggle to make ends meet and fall behind with household bills.

And experience with private insurance, to date, does not auger well for people living on low incomes. Many of the poorest people face difficulties obtaining private insurance to cover job loss and sickness or a private pension scheme at a price they could afford. This would include people with a history of unemployment, in insecure or part-time jobs or in low-paid self-employment, as well as many of those with a known illness or disability.

From October 1995, all new mortgage holders are being encouraged to take out private insurance cover to protect their mortgage payments for the first nine months following job loss. During that period they will receive no assistance from social security with their mortgage payments. People who took out mortgages before that date will receive no assistance for the first two months and only half their mortgage interest payments for the next four. It is too early for there to be any research on the effects of this change in rules. But if past experience with insurance claims is repeated, there is likely to be a large increase in mortgage arrears and possessions.

Experience with private insurance covering mortgage and loan payments following job loss or sickness has shown that insurance companies often failed to pay out when people tried to claim. In some cases there were clauses in the small print which policyholders were unaware of. One man, for example, had taken out insurance on a car loan, which he thought covered the repayments should either he or his wife need to give up work. He tried to claim when he had to give up work to care for his wife while she suffered from a mental illness. But he was turned down because the policy only covered him stopping work if he, himself, was ill.

I couldn't get a penny. The little red writing at the bottom, that nobody ever reads and I hadn't realised. I'd paid the insurance policy for two years.

He fell into arrears with the loan and his car was repossessed by the finance company.

In another case, a man had insurance to cover him for job loss following ill-health or disablement, but there was a dispute about how unfit he needed to be to be able to claim. He was asked to undergo a medical at which he was certified fit for limited work. The insurance company was only prepared to pay out if he had been found totally incapable of work.

I had an insurance that stated, if you were unable to do your own work, there would be a lump sum payment and £600 a month for 12 months, which would obviously have covered the mortgage. So I were blithely going along thinking, well if this is paid, financially I would have no problem. And then they suddenly move the goal posts. What they did, they altered conditions from 'you could do your own employment' to 'to do any type of work'. They sent me for a medical and wrote back and said 'You're able to do limited work'.

A third man had been sold a mortgage protection policy even though the insurance company knew he had an impairment. Yet when his disability forced him to give up work his claim was turned down on the grounds that the impairment nullified the policy.

These were not the only examples. Other people were either sold policies that did not cover them at all, because they failed from the outset to meet the criteria for the insurance, or had policies with exclusions that limited the payout when they needed to claim.

(Ford, 1994; Grant, 1995; Herbert and Kempson, 1995; Kempson *et al*, 1994).

Fraud

In addition to the drive to cut the costs of social security, there has been a well-publicised campaign to tackle fraud. It is, however, important to draw a distinction between three different types of fraud:

- organised fraud

- people who claim benefits while working full-time or living permanently with a partner

- people who work occasionally or have a partner to stay while claiming benefit.

Few people condone organised fraud. The qualitative research shows that most claimants also find fraud motivated by greed (for example people claiming Income Support while working full-time) less acceptable than that committed through need (taking casual work while claiming benefit). It also seems to be less common.

The research also identifies some of the reasons *why* people commit social security fraud. For example, lone mothers who continued to claim Income Support while living with a partner often had on-off relationships, with the man playing little role in the financial support of the family at any time. These women were reluctant to give up their financial independence.

> *[He's] bloody useless, can't leave the bairn with him or nothing. He never gives me any money when he's here. Just hangs around a while, then gets nasty, starts hitting me and leaves.*

In fact, domestic violence was fairly common in such on-off relationships.

In another case a lone mother was admitted to hospital for a mastectomy and asked her ex-husband to move into the house to look after their disabled son. They had been divorced for 13 years and led completely separate lives, but there was no-one else she could ask and she wanted to avoid having her son put into care. When she came out of hospital she was far from well so he stayed on to help her cope with the son. A neighbour reported her to the Benefits Agency and she was accused by them of fraudulently claiming £400 Income Support and £400 Housing Benefit and was repaying it at £4 a week. She felt she had been a victim of a terrible injustice.

The Social haven't understood. They couldn't care tuppence. They said 'Well it's not our fault you've had your breast off'. And I thought 'It's not ours either'. That's a woman at social security. She said it's not our problem, it's not our problem you've had your breast off.

Such cases show a lack of sensitivity and inflexibility that are worrying if they are widespread.

Quite a number of people work while claiming benefit and do not declare their earnings (see Chapter 4). But the research shows that the work people did was either casual (often a day or two at a time) or else it was a part-time job for a small number of hours each week. In both cases, they faced the prospect of effectively losing most of their earnings if they declared them or, in the case of casual work, the administrative problems associated with coming off benefit for just a week.

By and large, people did these jobs because they had financial problems. Home owners often did so to help make good shortfalls on their mortgage interest payments not covered by Income Support. In other cases, threats from a creditor had persuaded people to try to earn a little money. Christmas, too, encouraged some lone mothers to take on casual work, so that they could buy their children presents. In all these cases it was need rather than greed that led them to commit fraud.

There were also a small number of cases where people, especially those who were self-employed, had underdeclared their earnings on claims for Family Credit. Here there was less obvious justification for the fraud. Although none of them was especially well off, they were not in real need either.

(Ford *et al*, forthcoming; Grant, 1995; Herbert and Kempson, 1996; Kempson *et al*, 1994; Morris and Ritchie, 1994; Speak *et al*, 1995.)

Social security and social change

The social security system has been expected to pick up the costs of changes occurring in other areas of social and economic policy. At the same time, it has not always been adapted in line with general economic and social changes. Most of these changes have been covered in earlier chapters, but are summarised below.

Labour markets

The structure of the benefits system does not accommodate the sort of jobs that are on offer in the 'flexible' labour market. The main change has been the introduction of Family Credit for parents in low-paid work of 16 hours or more. This has improved the standard of living for many low-income families, but the possible widening of in-work benefits, through Earnings Top-ups for people without children, may well institutionalise low pay and create new poverty traps.

Moreover, many of the 'new' jobs on offer are only casual or for a few hours a week and are not adequately accommodated within the benefits system. Claimants can take these jobs, but must declare their earnings. Anything they earn above £5 a week (£15 for lone parents and £10 for couples who are long-term benefit claimants) is then deducted pound for pound from their benefit. As a consequence they are little better off financially for the work they do. It is this that encourages many not to declare their earnings and to run the risk of being apprehended for fraud.

(Ford *et al*, forthcoming; Kempson *et al*, 1994; Morris and Ritchie, 1994.)

Housing

Shifts in housing tenure, arising from government policy, have led to large numbers of low-paid home buyers who, unlike tenants with similar incomes, receive no assistance with their housing costs. This puts them at a high risk of falling behind with their mortgage repayments. In fact, many people who fell into arrears did so because their earnings had fallen. This has led to calls for a 'mortgage benefit' to help low-paid home buyers, which has found little favour with the government.

Moreover, widening home ownership, coupled with increasing job insecurity, has meant a growth in the numbers of home buyers losing their jobs and claiming social security. This has increased expenditure on mortgage assistance which led to the recent restrictions to its availability.

In the social rented sector, rent increases arising from a policy of moving towards market rents, and the shift from bricks and mortar subsidies, have increased the number of tenants who are eligible for Housing Benefit and potentially caught in the unemployment and poverty traps. They have also increased social security expenditure. The Housing Benefit taper was increased many times during the 1980s to cut back costs, and this increased the poverty trap for claimants. Changes to the taper also took some people outside the scope of Housing Benefit by reducing the level of income at which people qualified for assistance.

Deregulation of the private rented market has also pushed up rents, so that, despite taper changes, more tenants are eligible for Housing Benefit and now face the prospect of 'rent restrictions' and receiving assistance with only part of their rent.

(Ford, 1994; Ford *et al*, forthcoming; Kemp and McLaverty, 1995; Kempson *et al*, 1994.)

Care in the community
The social security system has had to pick up the some of the costs of care in the community. It has also been found to undermine that policy. Stroke victims leaving hospital were often unsure about their future income and faced delays in their assessment for benefit, which made it impossible for them to play a part in planning their own care. Single homeless people, including those with mental health problems or drug or alcohol dependencies, faced difficulties claiming Income Support.

Variations in the charges made by local authorities for care services mean that benefit claimants may get them free if they live in some areas or have to pay if they live in others. Those needing a substantial package of care are hit hardest as there is no allowance for these costs in benefit rates.

(Baldock and Ungerson, 1994; Bines, 1994; Grant, 1995; Griffiths, 1995; Pleace, 1995.)

Privatisation of utilities
Even privatisation of the utilities has brought discussion of the role to be played by social security in helping people on low incomes to pay for essential services. Since privatisation there have been growing regional variations in prices charged for water services, but benefit claimants receive a notional, unspecified amount that takes no account of regional differences. (For a while, water charges were not even included in the Rossi Index used to uprate means-tested benefits.) Growing regional differences in charges have led to suggestions that a 'water benefit' may be needed to compensate people living on low incomes in high water charge areas.

Regional price variations do not yet pose a problem with other utilities such as gas, electricity and telephones but, with growing competition, they may well do so in the future.

(Herbert and Kempson, 1995.)

Summary

Shifts from direct to indirect taxation have widened income inequalities, while reforms of local taxation (and the introduction of the Poll Tax in particular) have placed a further strain on the budgets of people living on low incomes.

Restraint on public expenditure has put the social security budget under constant scrutiny, with many changes taking place to try to contain spending. Since the early 1980s benefits and state pensions have, generally, been uprated in line with prices, which has meant that claimants' incomes have fallen behind those of the rest of the population. The late 1980s also saw substantial social security reforms, particularly to means-tested benefits and benefits for sick and disabled people. The overall aims of these reforms were to simplify the system, control spending and target payments on particular groups. Many of these changes have placed a greater emphasis on the use of discretion in determining entitlement.

Some of these changes, such as the replacement of Family Income Supplement by Family Credit, have improved the financial positions of the claimants entitled to them. Others, including the removal of entitlement to Income Support for 16 and 17 year olds and the introduction of the Social Fund to replace single payments, have made life more difficult.

Besides the introduction of new benefits, there have been important changes to the ways that benefits have been administered. Housing Benefit administration was transferred to local authorities, Statutory Sick Pay and Maternity Pay to employers, and a range of agencies set up to administer various aspects of social security at 'arm's length' from the Department of Social Security. In some instances there were problems at the time of the transfer, but most changes have, on balance, improved the service to claimants.

Other administrative changes have not always been so beneficial for claimants, including the decision to pay most benefits fortnightly and in arrears, and the increased use of direct payments from benefit. The provision of information and advice by the Benefits Agency and non-take-up of benefit are two areas where progress has been made, but much still remains to be done.

A number of topics tend to be uppermost in the debate about social security. There is a continuing concern to contain expenditure on social security, focusing on ways of targeting it on those in greatest need; reducing dependence on the state and increasing work incentives; and exploring an increased role for private insurance and pensions. Closely linked to this is the well-publicised campaign to reduce levels of social security fraud. Finally, there is the relationship between social security and wider social and economic changes on the one hand and other areas of social and economic policy on the other. There is a growing concern about the extent to which the social security system is being expected to accommodate the costs of changes in the labour and housing markets, the policy of care in the community, and even the privatisation of utilities. This concern is reinforced because the changes often result in an even closer scrutiny of the social security budget, so that it is frequently the very poorest households who suffer most.

PART THREE

8 Conclusions and policy implications

One thing is clear from the analysis in this report – people who live on low incomes are not an underclass. They have aspirations just like others in society: they want a job; a decent home; and an income that is enough to pay the bills with a little to spare. But social and economic changes that have benefited the majority of the population, increasing their incomes and their standard of living, have made life more difficult for a growing minority, whose fairly modest aspirations are often beyond their reach.

Finding and keeping a job

Most people view a job as the only way they can secure an adequate income. They do not want hand-outs or to be dependent on the State, but to be able to provide for themselves and their families. But people are not equal in the job market.

Global competition has enabled most people to improve their standard of living, by reducing the price of consumer goods either through cheaper labour costs in the emerging economies or through cheaper production costs resulting from the introduction of new technology. But these changes have created a very restricted job market for unskilled and semi-skilled workers, for whom both wages and job security are declining. This shift has been further fuelled by deregulation within the British labour market.

At the same time, discrimination in the labour market means that certain groups tend to be more hit by these shifts than others: young people with no work experience; older workers; ethnic minorities; and people who are sick or disabled.

There is, as a result, a growing group of people who have not had 'a proper job' for years and can see no prospect of getting one in the future. Statistics show that most unemployed people do not remain out of work for long periods. But the qualitative research reveals an alternation between unemployment and low-paid work, with no real escape from life on a low income. Instead individuals and families find themselves moving from low to very low incomes and back to low again.

Policy responses to these changes have tended to concentrate on supply rather than demand factors – increasing work incentives and offering retraining. There have been many changes to increase work incentives (see Chapter 4), yet the qualitative research shows that this is not the main problem. Most people want to work and go to great lengths to find a job, especially if they are the main breadwinner in the household. But they face a number of barriers to achieving adequate incomes through work

Lack of jobs

There is a shortage of jobs, especially for unskilled and semi-skilled workers. Training is an important way of tackling such a mismatch of skills and there have been a series of initiatives in this area.

The 1988 social security reforms withdrew entitlement to benefit for 16 and 17 year olds, but offered them the guarantee of a place on a training scheme. In practice, training places are *not*, however, always available and Chapter 7 shows the hardship that ensues – especially where family relationships break down and young people leave home. The Training Guarantee should be honoured, and where it is not there is a clear case for more 16 and 17 year olds to be entitled to benefit.

There have also been a number of government initiatives over the past 15 years that have offered retraining for unemployed workers. However, as Chapter 4 shows, there is a growing cynicism about these schemes that needs to be addressed.

Moreover, the research reviewed for this report also suggests that tackling supply alone is inadequate and that active labour market policies are needed which will tackle demand as well.

Low pay

Recent trends have been towards the creation of low-paid, part-time or temporary jobs, paying wages that just about cover bills and offer subsistence living. People who are reluctant to take these jobs are being encouraged to lower their wage expectations – sometimes to bare subsistence levels – or have their benefit reduced. Yet Chapters 2 and 3 show all too clearly the consequences for people living long-term on very low incomes and suggest that Jobcentre staff need a clearer understanding of the levels of income that people require.

Unemployed people's wage aspirations are generally modest. They want to be able to cover all their bills, afford a relatively healthy diet, to heat their homes and replace their clothing when needed and, ideally, to have a little left over to put by for a rainy day and allow them to lead a life that is more than bare essentials. Moreover, they want to do so without having to claim in-work benefits. Typically they say they need about £20–30 a week on top of their outgoings to relieve the sorts of worries and deprivations that currently characterise lives on low incomes. As Chapter 4 has shown, this means net weekly incomes of:

- £150 for single householders

- £175 for couples without children

- £180 for a lone parent with two children

- £200 for couples with two or three children.

The crucial question is how these levels of income can be best achieved. There are two very different approaches to ensuring minimum incomes for those who have jobs: in-work benefits and a minimum wage.

In-work benefits, like Family Credit and the experimental Earnings Top-ups, increase people's incomes, but they run the risk of institutionalising low pay – and public spending ends up effectively subsidising unscrupulous or unsuccessful employers. They also trap claimants in high marginal tax rates, making it difficult for them to increase their incomes through additional work. In fact, resistance to claiming in-work benefits accentuates the effects of the unemployment trap, as people look for wages that would enable them to cover their housing costs and other bills from their earnings. Failure to claim in-work benefit entitlement increases hardship.

On the other hand, a minimum wage approach is largely about equity in the labour market and, alone, is unlikely to solve the problem of family poverty. Chapter 4 shows that to come close to people's income aspirations a minimum wage of around £4.75 an hour would be required – assuming current tax, National Insurance and Child Benefit levels. This may prove to be unrealistic and likely to heighten worries about the risk of damaging employment creation.

In reality a combination of these two approaches may prove to be the most viable way of ensuring adequate incomes in work. In any case they need to be considered in conjunction with levels of Child Benefit and tax allowances and tax and National Insurance rates.

Temporary and part-time jobs

People are expected to be flexible in their approach to the job market, taking temporary and short-term jobs, and those offering a few hours work a week. But the social security system, as it stands, is not flexible enough to accommodate these jobs. People who take them benefit very littl financially, unless they commit fraud. As the *Inquiry into Income and Wealth* concluded, an official review is needed to identify how the social security system can adapt to the flexible labour market and enable people to help themselves.

There are a number of ways of achieving this increased flexibility that might be considered:

- increasing the sources of income that are not affected by work status to provide a secure income floor for those moving off benefit and into work. These might include increased Child Benefit (paid for by abolishing the married couple's tax allowance); subsidised childcare; maintenance disregard; and separate benefits (or a 'benefit disregard') for partners

- increasing the level of Income Support earnings disregards to permit people who work fewer than 16 hours a week to retain more of their earnings

- extending the period over which earnings disregards are calculated to accommodate casual work

- smoothing the transition between work and benefits by reducing delays in processing benefit. Recent changes, such as the four week run-on of full Housing Benefit for people moving into work, are a welcome development

- more assistance with costs of attending interviews and Social Fund (or other) help with costs of returning to work.

Tackling non-financial barriers to work.

Not all of the barriers to people working are financial. Lone parents frequently delay their return to work through a lack of suitable childcare – not just for under-fives but for their school-age children too.

Older workers, people from ethnic minorities and sick and disabled people often face discrimination when looking for work. Legislation is only part of the solution; enforcement and other positive steps are needed to ensure equal access to work.

A decent home

People want a home that is affordable, large enough for their needs, in a reasonable state of repair, and in an area where fears of crime and vandalism do not dominate their lives. Yet changes in housing policy have meant that a growing number of people are unable to achieve these aspirations.

Need for rented housing

There is a clear need for a larger 'affordable' rented sector, with a wider mix of tenants in individual neighbourhoods.

The sale of council houses and low levels of new building have restricted access to the social rented sector; while deregulation of the private rented sector has led to large increases in rents. The consequences of these policies are described in Chapter 5. Vulnerable groups often cannot be found suitable accommodation, and those who are allocated new tenancies are often housed in less desirable properties (that others did not want to buy), in neighbourhoods with high levels of crime and vandalism. At the extreme, people become homeless. The research shows how poor housing (and more still homelessness) adds to the problems of living on a low income, affecting people's physical and mental health.

Changes in housing subsidies

The moves from bricks and mortar subsidies of social rented housing to near-market rents and greater reliance on means-tested benefits have led to more tenants becoming eligible for Housing Benefit. *The Inquiry into Income and Wealth* concluded that 'this switch has gone too far' and Chapter 5 of this report shows its consequences.

Rising rents have increased the unemployment trap for many tenants. This is partly through lack of knowledge about Housing Benefit for those in work and partly through a resistance to claiming benefit while working. As a consequence, some people live in poverty because they do not claim the Housing Benefit to which they are entitled.

Meanwhile, higher rents have also led to growing expenditure on Housing Benefit and to moves to contain spending – by reducing the numbers of people eligible, by altering the income and savings rules, and by restrictions on the amount of rent covered by Housing Benefit in the private rented sector. People who have little or no bargaining power are being expected to negotiate lower rents or find somewhere cheaper to live.

Limits to home ownership

Deregulation of the mortgage markets and giving tenants the 'right to buy' their council homes at a discount have enabled a wider group of households to realise their dream of owning a home. But for some that dream has turned into a nightmare. The evidence in this report suggests that, without better safeguards for low-income and unemployed home buyers, the limits of home ownership have been reached.

Growing job insecurity means that some people can no longer afford to buy a home without running the risk of mortgage arrears and possessions. The risks for newer entrants to home ownership (young people and manual workers) are especially great. Recent changes to the Income Support 'safety net' will increase the risk of arrears and possessions for home buyers who lose their jobs, unless the private insurance industry provides adequate and affordable alternative cover. There have also been many calls for a mortgage benefit for low-waged home buyers in the same way as Housing Benefit supports those who rent. Certainly any further widening of home ownership, drawing in more low-paid buyers, would be ill advised without such a benefit.

Recent house price falls have left substantial numbers of people with negative equity. Mortgage lenders are developing packages to enable people in this position to move home and trade down, but more remains to be done. Because mortgage arrears and negative equity are frequently linked, home ownership has been a route into homelessness and long-term poverty for several hundred thousand households. The costs to these households are spelt out graphically by the qualitative research. A larger, more affordable rented sector would assist people in this position, as would more flexible approaches to tenure, allowing people to change tenure while remaining in the same home.

An adequate income

There will always be some people on low incomes who, because of age, disability or family circumstances, will remain dependent on social security for their income and who will not benefit from higher wages and more employment opportunities. To cut them adrift from rising living standards would be cynically to exploit their disadvantage and powerlessness.

While most people on low incomes dream of winning the pools or the lottery, in reality their aspirations are, as already seen, a great deal more modest. Yet, the qualitative research shows that people living on benefit usually have insufficient income to cover even their basic needs. As a consequence they face a difficult choice between paying their bills on time and having adequate food and heating. Chapter 3 shows that as little as £15 extra a week can make a great deal of difference to the ability of people living on Income Support to pay their bills without needing to forgo essentials. There are a number of ways in which this modest amount could be achieved.

Reversing the growth in income inequalities

While average incomes have increased over the past 15 years, changes to taxation and benefits have led to growing income inequalities. Using government statistics, the *Inquiry into Income and Wealth* showed that, after allowing for housing costs, average incomes increased by 36 per cent between 1979 and 1991/2. But while the real income of the top tenth grew over this period by around 60 per cent, people in the poorest tenth in 1991/2 saw no significant increase in their incomes compared with those of the equivalent group in 1979.

Had the link between earnings and levels of social security payments not been broken, many benefit claimants would now have the additional £15 claimants need to avoid real financial hardship. Growing numbers of people, through no fault of their own, either remain on benefit or alternate between low wages and benefit for substantial periods of time. In such cases price indexation of benefits and state pensions is inadequate and benefits should increase by more than inflation when general living standards are rising.

Income tax changes, meanwhile, have benefited the rich far more than the poor; and increases in VAT have a bigger impact the lower a household's income. Future tax changes should lessen the tax burden borne by those with low incomes.

Revising the benefits system

Many of the changes that would make it easier for people to move into work could also increase the incomes of people who remain on benefit for long periods of time. These include:

- increasing the weekly amount that can be earned without loss of Income Support to £15 a week for all claimants, and/or allowing income to be disregarded over a longer period of time

- a 15 a week maintenance disregard, permitting women claiming Income Support to retain a little of the money they receive from ex-partners

- an increase in Child Benefit, by phasing out the married couple's tax allowance

- the retention of insurance-based benefits that preserve incentives for partners of claimants to work.

There is also room for revising the benefits system to make it both simpler for claimants and easier and cheaper to administer. Currently large numbers of people fail to claim the benefit to which they are entitled, with average weekly amounts unclaimed being in excess of £20.

At the same time, fine tuning of the rules of entitlement leads to high administrative costs, the need to respond to frequent changes in claimants' circumstances, and to delays and errors that cause hardship to claimants. Six-monthly reassessments of minor changes affecting entitlement to Housing Benefit or Council Tax Benefit, for example, might lead to some rough justice but, if the resulting savings were used to increase the level of benefit, could lead to more cost-effectiveness.

Social security and wider social and economic change

The way that the social security system is being expected to pick up the costs of wider social and economic changes needs to be reviewed (see Chapter 7). Some of these changes, such as the growing numbers of lone parents and pensioners, are hard to prevent. But others have resulted from shifts in policy. As the *Inquiry into Income and Wealth* concluded:

> *Too many spending decisions have been compartmentalised, with apparent savings being made by one department, agency or company, only to rebound on another, often the Department of Social Security, and with short-term cash restraints acting as the sole criterion for decision-making.*

> *Economic policies* of government and employers have increased the numbers of people who claim social security because they cannot find work. This, in turn, has led to restrictions which have reduced the numbers of unemployed and sick or disabled people eligible for insurance-based benefits and a tightening of the criteria for benefit entitlement generally.

> *Shifts in housing* subsidies have led to a large increase in Housing Benefit expenditure, which has, in turn, led to a series of measures designed to cut the budget.

Encouragement of low-income home ownership at a time of growing job insecurity has increased Income Support expenditure on assistance with mortgage interest payments. This, in turn, has led to restrictions in the availability of state assistance and an encouragement of private insurance provision.

The policy of care in the community has shifted costs from the health service to the social security and local authority budgets. At the same time, controls on local authority spending mean that many people now have to contribute to the costs of assistance that they would previously have received free. In some local authorities this even extends to Income Support claimants having to pay for care services such as day care and home helps.

Privatisation of the former public utilities has brought a more commercial approach to their services. Pricing policies have, until now, included cross-subsidies which have, generally, benefited low-income customers. Changes in pricing policy will inevitably mean poor consumers paying more. British Gas has already introduced reduced tariffs for people who pay by standing order, while electricity and gas consumers with pre-payment meters pay a higher than average tariff. Water charges have increased substantially since privatisation, with wide regional variations. Re-balancing of tariffs for other utilities would result in people in rural areas paying more for their supplies. It is widely believed, in the privatised utilities, that cross-subsidies should be phased out and the social security system should ensure that people are able to pay their bills.

Many of these changes have been designed to cut overall public spending and to deliver a higher standard of living to the majority of the population. In the process they have increased social security expenditure and led to demands for this spending to be contained. It is those living on the lowest incomes who ultimately pay the price.

Tackling the problems faced by people on low incomes will require greater co-ordination in key areas of policy, with more consideration of the wider consequences of policy change. Such co-ordination needs to cover not just government departments, but all public and private bodies whose policies have a direct impact on the lives of poor people.

Making ends meet

People living on low incomes show great resilience and resourcefulness as they try to make ends meet. As Chapters 1–3 show, managing a limited amount of money requires great skill: costing and controlling a tight budget; setting priorities; juggling bills; making difficult choices; cutting out all but the essentials and sometimes going without these necessities too. Women, who generally manage the budget, bear the brunt of these continual worries. Learning these skills takes time and practice and not everyone succeeds in managing well – or, at least, not quickly enough to avoid financial difficulties. This is hardly surprising, since people on low incomes are as varied as others in more fortunate circumstances. A minority use a 'pay-as-you-go' approach, neither planning ahead nor recording their outgoings. With an adequate income this approach causes few serious problems, but with no margin for error, it frequently leads to debt.

In general, avoiding debt is more a matter of experience and practice making ends meet than of attitudes to paying bills. People 'learn from doing'– and sometimes from costly mistakes. There may be no alternative to this cruel university of life, but improved tuition at school and more ready access to money advice before serious problems occur could well help.

Although most people keep the bailiff at bay, their poverty has wider consequences. Making ends meet on a low income means going without. Spending on food is reduced and diets tend to be high in fat and low in vitamin C and other key nutrients. Similarly, fuel bills are kept to a minimum by restricting the use of heating and hot water, even on very cold days. While people appear to cope better the longer they have been on low incomes, living in poverty can take a long-term toll on their physical and mental health. Even the most carefully managed budget is precarious. Relatively small hiccoughs – a larger than expected bill, children requiring new shoes, or a household appliance breaking down – are enough to cause problems as there is usually so little room for manoeuvre.

Giving more control to claimants

Exercising very tight financial control is a vital part of making ends meet on a low income. Yet a number of administrative changes have left benefit claimants with less control over their money – in striking contrast to the general thrust of government policies which aim to give people greater freedom of choice about how to spend their money. For example:

- The payment of most benefits fortnightly in arrears causes problems for people who operate tight weekly budgets.

- The low availability of grants from the Social Fund results in many people facing genuine need not taking out loans because they cannot afford to repay them from their weekly benefit. Others do borrow from the Fund, but have even less to live on as a consequence.

- The increasing use of direct payments from benefit to creditors who are owed money is welcomed by some people, but others find it restricts their room for juggling when they face an emergency or unexpected expenditure. In some cases, the deductions are so high that people cannot cover their basic needs. Although higher levels of deduction can only be made with the claimant's agreement, in practice many do not feel they have a choice.

- The growing use of discretion in determining eligibility for benefits can mean that people in similar circumstances do not receive the same amount of financial assistance.

Individually, none of these would necessarily cause serious problems, but combined with basic incomes that offer no room for manoeuvre they frequently do.

Combating exclusion

Increasing choice for the majority has, undoubtedly, narrowed the options for a sizeable minority of people who live on low incomes. Moreover, most of the changes discussed in this report have affected the same groups of people. Those who are out of work or have low-paid jobs have seen their incomes grow least because of fiscal and social security changes. They have the most limited access to housing and financial services, and are hit hardest by rises in basic household bills. They represent a sizeable minority of people who, through no fault of their own, are being effectively marginalised.

Social exclusion
Social activities are the first to be sacrificed as people attempt to make ends meet on a low income. Poverty is a source of stigma and shame that causes many to cut themselves off from friends and a social life. As far as possible parents try to protect their children from this social exclusion, but many children are unable to participate in school trips or other social activities with their school friends.

Low-income families, through necessity, spend long periods in one another's company. Constant money problems can either cement their relationships (usually those that are already strong) or help destroy them, sometimes resulting in family breakdown and divorce.

Homelessness and marginalised areas

While most people are adequately housed, there has been a long-term upward trend in street homelessness – often affecting vulnerable people, so that poor health and homelessness become inextricably linked. Homeless people face a poverty cycle of 'no home, no job; no job, no home', which requires concerted efforts to be broken.

Housing policy has also led to the concentration of high unemployment, low incomes and lone parenthood in particular neighbourhoods and on particular housing estates. High levels of crime and vandalism add greatly to the problems people already face. They become afraid to go out, live in fear and face a high risk of their possessions being stolen or destroyed. It is possible to revitalise these areas, given the will and resources to do so.

Financial exclusion

Most people have benefited greatly from the development of services provided by financial institutions following deregulation. More sophisticated screening of applicants, however, means a small minority of people either have no access to these services or find they do not cater for those who need to keep close control over their money. Where alternatives are available, they usually involve additional costs. People without bank accounts face charges for cashing cheques or making payments through post offices, and are unable to take advantage of reduced tariffs for paying bills on direct debit. Loans from local moneylenders cost considerably more than credit from high street financial institutions. And people living in high crime neighbourhoods are often denied access even to licensed moneylenders and frequently have no option but to turn to unlicensed loan sharks and pay huge financial and other costs.

Exclusion from the consumer society

Inadequate incomes and lack of access to high street consumer credit mean people cannot acquire consumer goods and services that most people take for granted. The pressures of a consumer society are not lessened by living on a low income and are especially felt by younger people, who are faced with the costs of setting up home and with the persuasive strategies and demands of children.

Offering hope for the future

Many of the people interviewed for the research reviewed in this report were well aware of how restricted their lives were. Short of winning the lottery or the pools they could see little hope for the future.

More worrying, unlike previous generations they saw little hope of things getting better for their children. Reversing this trend of growing exclusion is, therefore, one of the greatest challenges facing society, which calls for responses from a wide range of organisations – including central government, local authorities and commercial companies.

Governments undoubtedly have less control over the economy and labour market than was once the case – although they have greater freedom of manoeuvre than they sometimes care to admit. Unemployment and the widening dispersion of incomes from work are the factors that have contributed most to the number of people living on low incomes and the hardship they experience. It follows, therefore, that a commitment to full employment and a reluctance deliberately to use unemployment as an economic regulator are prerequisites for any comprehensive strategy to improve the lot of people living on a low income. So, too, are policies to tackle low pay and ensure that tax changes do not increase the tax burden of those least able to pay.

Even with a policy of full employment, there will be some people who have to rely on financial support from the state. The level at which this income is set will, in part, determine the extent to which they are excluded from the quality of life and choices that others take for granted. It is important that people in this position are allowed to benefit from general rises in prosperity and are not penalised by attempts to reduce the burden of tax for those who are better off. Central government also has an important part to play in ensuring an adequate supply of affordable rented housing for people who are unable, or would be ill-advised, to buy a home for themselves.

As more essential services are privatised, it is important to ensure that people are not denied access to them through lack of income. An unquestioning belief in free markets can lead to a mistaken assumption that everyone has access. Private companies which supply those essential services should be aware of the impact of their decisions on people with low incomes and not assume that the State will pick up the cost. The government should also take steps to protect the most vulnerable through the regulatory system and by ensuring an adequate income. Local authorities, too, have an important part to play: in economic regeneration; housing improvement and tackling the problems of hard-to-let estates; providing free care services to those in need; ensuring that transport, cultural and leisure services remain affordable for people on low incomes; and encouraging welfare benefits and money advice services.

Re-establishing hope in the lives of people who live on low incomes requires co-ordinated policies on a number of fronts. But most of all it requires political courage: the courage to interpret 'One Nation Toryism', or 'A Stakeholder Economy' to mean that poverty can no longer be tolerated nor the poor forgotten. To do otherwise would be a tragic waste of human resources.

References

Items marked with an asterisk are the reports from the 31 core qualitative studies that have been reviewed in this report. For more details of any of these reports, see the Appendix.

* I Anderson and J Morgan, *Housing options for low-income single people: local authority and housing association policy and practice*. Centre for Housing Policy, University of York (Forthcoming).

* I Anderson and D Quilgars, *Foyers for young people: evaluation of a pilot initiative*. Centre for Housing Policy, University of York, 1995.

* J Baldock and C Ungerson, *Becoming consumers of community care: households within the mixed economy of welfare*. Joseph Rowntree Foundation, 1994.

R Berthoud and E Kempson, *Credit and debt*. Policy Studies Institute, 1992.

*W Bines, *The health of single homeless people*. Centre for Housing Policy, University of York, 1994 (Discussion Paper 9).

*L Burghes and M Brown, *Single lone mothers: problems, prospects and policies*. Family Policy Studies Centre, 1995.

*J Carlisle, *Housing needs of ex-prisoners*. Centre for Housing Policy, University of York (Forthcoming).

Child Support Agency, *Annual report 1994/5*. HMSO, 1995.

*K Clarke, C Glendinning and G Craig, *Small change: the Child Support Act two years on*. Family Policy Studies Centre, 1996.

A D H Crook, J Hughes and P Kemp, *The supply of privately rented homes: today and tomorrow*. Joseph Rowntree Foundation, 1995.

*B Dobson, A Beardsworth, T Keil and R Walker, *Diet, choice and poverty: social, cultural and nutritional aspects of food consumption among low-income families*. Family Policy Studies Centre, 1994.

*E Dowler and C Calvert, *Nutrition and diet in lone-parent families in London*. Family Policy Studies Centre, 1995.

*A Etherington, B Stocker and A Whittaker, *Outside but not inside – yet*. People First, 1995.

M Evans, *Not granted? An assessment of the change from single payments to the Social Fund*. STICERD, London School of Economics, 1994.

M Evans, D Piachaud and H Sutherland, *Designed for the poor – poorer by design: effects of the 1986 Social Security Act on family incomes*. STICERD, London School of Economics, 1994.

*J Ford, *Problematic home ownership: the management, experience and consequences of arrears and possessions in a depressed housing market*. Department of Social Studies, Loughborough University, 1994.

*J Ford, E Kempson and J England, *Housing, housing benefits and work disincentives*. Department of Social Studies, Loughborough University and Policy Studies Institute (Forthcoming).

*R Forrest, T Kennett and P Leather, *Home owners in negative equity*. School of Advanced Urban Studies, University of Bristol, 1994.

A Gosling, S Machin and C Meghir, *What's happened to wages?* (IFS Commentary No 43) and *The changing distribution of wages in the UK 1966 to 1992* (IFS Working Paper No 94/10). Institute for Fiscal Studies, 1994.

*L Grant, *Disability and debt: the experience of disabled people in debt*. Sheffield Citizen's Advice Bureaux Debt Support Unit, 1995.

P Gregg and J Wadsworth, *More work in fewer households?* National Institute of Economic and Social Research, 1995.

*S Griffiths, *Supporting community care: the contribution of housing benefit*. National Institute for Social Work, 1995.

R Hancock and P Weir, *More ways than means: a guide to pensioners' incomes during the 1980s*. Age Concern Institute of Gerontology, Kings College London, 1994.

*A Herbert and E Kempson, *Water debt and disconnection*. Policy Studies Institute, 1995.

*A Herbert and E Kempson, *Credit use among ethnic minorities*. Policy Studies Institute, 1996.

A Holmans, *Housing demand and need in England 1991–2011*. Joseph Rowntree Foundation, 1995.

*G Jones, *Family support for young people*. Family Policy Studies Centre, 1995.

*G Jones, *Leaving home*. Open University Press, 1995.

Joseph Rowntree Foundation, *Inquiry into income and wealth*. JRF, 1995 (2 vols).

*P Kemp and P McLaverty, *Private tenants and restrictions in rent for housing benefit*. Centre for Housing Policy, University of York, 1995.

*E Kempson, A Bryson and K Rowlingson, *Hard times? How poor families make ends meet*. Policy Studies Institute, 1994.

*I Law, C Hylton, A Karmani and A Deacon, *Racial equality and social security service delivery: a study of the perceptions and experiences of black minority ethnic people eligible for benefit in Leeds*. University of Leeds, 1994 (Sociology and Social Policy Research Working Paper 10).

N Meager, G Court and J Moralee, *Self-employment and the distribution of income*. Institute of Employment Studies, 1994.

G Meen, *The impact of higher rents*. Joseph Rowntree Foundation, 1994 (Housing Research Findings 109).

*S Middleton, K Ashworth and R Walker, *Family fortunes: pressures on parents and children in the 1990s*. Child Poverty Action Group, 1994.

*L Morris and J Ritchie, *Income maintenance and living standards*. Social and Community Planning Research, 1994.

*N Pleace, *Housing vulnerable single homeless people*. Centre for Housing Policy, University of York, 1995.

*A Power and R Tunstall, *Swimming against the tide: polarisation or progress on 20 unpopular council estates, 1980–1995.* Joseph Rowntree Foundation, 1995.

*C Roaf and C Lloyd, *Multi-agency work with young people in difficulty?* Oxford Brookes University, 1995.

*K Rowlingson, *Moneylenders and their customers.* Policy Studies Institute, 1994.

*J Rugg and L Sanderling, *Evaluation of access schemes.* Centre for Housing Policy, University of York (Forthcoming).

*M Shucksmith, P Chapman and G Clark, *Disadvantage in rural Scotland: how is it experienced and how can it be tackled? Summary report.* Rural Forum, 1995.

*S Speak, S Cameron, R Woods and R Gilroy, *Young single mothers: barriers to independent living.* Family Policy Studies Centre, 1995.

*H Third, *Affordable childcare and housing: a case study of tenants of a black housing association.* Centre for Housing Policy, University of York, 1995.

S Wilcox, *Housing finance review 1994/5.* Joseph Rowntree Foundation, 1994.

S Wilcox, *Housing finance review 1995/6.* Joseph Rowntree Foundation, 1995.

Appendix

I Anderson and J Morgan, *Housing options for low-income single people: local authority and housing association policy and practice*, Centre for Housing Policy, University of York (Forthcoming).

A study of housing provision for single people through local authorities and housing associations. Through an analysis of policy documents, a telephone survey and pluralistic case studies, the research has looked at policy and practice regarding low-income single people, aged between 16 and 59, who are homeless or in housing need.

Findings: Forthcoming

I Anderson and D Quilgars, *Foyers for young people: evaluation of a pilot initiative* Centre for Housing Policy, University of York, 1995.

The French *Foyers* were recognised as a possible model for tackling youth homelessness and unemployment in Britain. In 1992, a pilot, consisting of seven foyers/hostels, was set up as one of a number of initiatives designed to help young people break out of the cycle of 'no home, no job, no home'. This independent evaluation monitored their progress for the whole of the pilot period (January 1992 to March 1994). This involved depth interviews with key personnel, interviews with young people using the services and a survey of employers involved with the pilot foyers, as well as monitoring the characteristics of users, attendance at liaison meetings and the collection of background data.

Findings: HR 142 *Foyers for young people*

J Baldock and C Ungerson, *Becoming consumers of community care: households within the mixed economy of welfare*. Joseph Rowntree Foundation,1994.

Faced with the new mixed economy of care, how do newly dependent people view the services they receive and are they able to participate in decisions about their care? A six-month follow-up study of 32 older people returning to the community after surviving a stroke showed considerable obstacles to successful care management and to the 'mixed economy' of care. Most did not know the names of key care organisers and had only a vague perception that they were 'care managed'. Mixing public and private services was problematic and the people interviewed did not understand how they related to one another. In each case the elderly person and their carer was interviewed three times over the six-month period following discharge from hospital.

Findings: SCR 55 *User perceptions of a 'mixed economy' of care*

W Bines, *The health of single homeless people.* Centre for Housing Policy, University of York, 1994 (Discussion Paper 9).

Single homeless people experience worse physical and mental health than the general population; and among those who are homeless, those sleeping rough have more health problems than those living in hostels. Heavy drinking and alcohol-related problems were also more of a problem among those sleeping rough than they were for hostel residents. Although most single homeless people wanted their own home, a high proportion of those with health problems needed support – advice, help with housekeeping or social work support. In addition to secondary analysis of data from a national survey of homeless people and the British Household Panel Survey, the study included 20 group discussions. In these discussions, single homeless people were encouraged to talk about their physical and mental health as well as other aspects of their lives.

Findings: HR 128 *The health of single homeless people*

L Burghes and M Brown, *Single lone mothers: problems, prospects and policies.* Family Policy Studies Centre, 1995.

Single lone mothers are more common now than 20 years ago, rising five-fold to just under 500,000. Through desk research, this study set out to explore the demographic development of all single mothers and their socio-economic circumstances. This was complemented by depth interviews with 31 mothers who, at conception, were teenagers and had never been married. These explored the mothers' expectations and experiences of relationships and family life. They showed that young single motherhood was neither planned nor advocated by those who experienced it, and experiences were often at odds with the mothers' past expectations and future hopes for a more 'traditional' family life. Most faced difficulties obtaining housing; family support was not always forthcoming; and most struggled to get by on Income

Support. Most preferred to remain at home with their children, but those who wanted to work part-time were thwarted by limited opportunities and a lack of childcare.

Findings: SPR 84 *Single lone mothers*

J Carlisle, *Housing needs of ex-prisoners.* Centre for Housing Policy, University of York (Forthcoming).

Each year about 90,000 people are released from prisons in England and Wales and fewer than half of them are able to return to the accommodation they lived in before they went to prison. 175 prisoners were interviewed shortly before their release and, of these, 49 were re-interviewed between four and eight months later. In addition, 23 professionals whose jobs involved helping prisoners with accommodation problems were also interviewed. Together these interviews provide a disturbing picture of the housing problems faced on release from prison. Only prisoners who had previously lived in local authority housing had a low risk of losing their home. Little was done by professionals to prevent people losing their homes and those who had kept them largely did so through help from friends and family. Benefit rules meant that home owners were almost certain to have their homes repossessed and recent Housing Benefit changes mean that social tenants, too, will be likely to end up homeless in future.

Findings: Forthcoming

K Clarke, C Glendinning and G Craig, *Small change: the Child Support Act two years on.* Family Policy Studies Centre, 1996.

The 1991 Child Support Act is an important piece of recent family legislation because of the impact is has on some hitherto private areas of family life and responsibilities and the controversy surrounding its implementation. This study is part of a three-stage longitudinal evaluation of the medium-term effects of the Child Support Act on lone mothers and their children, who were in receipt of Income Support or family Credit at the time the act was implemented. It was based on depth interviews: with 29 lone mothers in March 1993, just before the Act came into effect; with 54 mothers one year later; and with 53 mothers two years after the Act came into effect. The last wave of interviews is the subject of this report. It shows that, while many mothers welcomed the setting up of the Child Support Agency, many were a good deal more equivocal two years later.

Findings: Forthcoming

B Dobson, A Beardsworth, T Keil and R Walker, *Diet, choice and poverty: Social, cultural and nutritional aspects of food consumption among low-income families.* Family Policy Studies Centre, 1994.

When money is short, food is one of the few options low-income households have for cutting back their spending. Using detailed case studies this study explores the process by which 48 low-income families (half of them lone parents) decided what foods to eat. Each case study comprised four elements: individual interviews; expenditure diaries; consumption diaries; and combined interviews with all members of the family, where possible. Together, these explored how people adapted to the experience of eating on a low income and why they made particular choices about buying food. All the families studied managed to get enough to eat but such 'success' was achieved at a price, such as self-denial, family stress and unwelcome changes in diet and shopping habits.

Findings: SP 66 *Eating on a low income*

E Dowler and C Calvert, *Nutrition and diet in lone-parent families in London.* Family Policy Studies Centre, 1995.

Cutting back on food is one of the least visible aspects of poverty, yet one with potentially damaging effects on health and well-being. This study of the diets of lone parents and their children investigated the nutritional consequences of the strategies that lone parents adopted where money was tight and food choice constrained. However careful the poorest lone parents were about budgeting and shopping for food, their nutrient intakes were always lower and their diets less healthy than those who were not poor. Nutrition data were obtained from individual 3-day food intake records for 131 lone parents and at least one of their children, and from a food frequency questionnaire. Semi-structured interviews in 200 lone parent households examined household budgeting and management in relation to food and health.

Findings: SP 71 *Diets of lone parents*

A Etherington, B Stocker and A Whittaker, *Outside but not inside – yet.* People First, 1995.

Community care legislation means that more people with learning difficulties are moving out of hospital to live in the community. This study sought the views of some of those leaving institutional care, looking at the ways they were helped to leave hospital and what their lives are like in the community. Interviews were held with 34 people with learning difficulties and 28 care staff. These found that people leaving hospital want more choice about where they live and how they spend their days (most went to a day centre). In addition they would find it helpful to get more training about the new kinds of skills they need if they are to get the most out of living in the community.

Findings: SCR 64 *Moving from hospital into the community: an evaluation by people with learning difficulties*

J Ford, Problematic home ownership: the management, experience and consequences of arrears and possessions in a depressed housing market. Department of Social Studies, Loughborough University, 1994.

The continuing number of mortgage arrears and possessions is an important legacy of the late 1980s housing boom. This study identifies the changing management of arrears in the early 1990s, and explores the continuing social and financial consequences of the arrears and possessions process for households and housing providers. It drew on an interview survey of over 1,200 owner occupiers in Glasgow, Luton and Bristol, analysing the responses of those living in Luton and Bristol who were in arrears. In addition, 16 people who had lost their homes were interviewed in depth and the court records of mortgage possession cases in the Luton and Bristol courts were analysed in detail.

Findings: HR 125 *The consequences of mortgage arrears and possessions in a depressed housing market*

J Ford, E Kempson and J England, *Housing, housing benefits and work disincentives.* Department of Social Studies and Policy Studies Institute, Loughborough University (Forthcoming).

A depth interview study to investigate the role that housing costs and assistance with housing costs play in decisions regarding work. Forty interviews are being undertaken with home owners and tenants who are living on either Income Support or low earnings. They include a range of household types, including single people, couples with no dependent children, lone parents and couples with dependent children.

Findings: Forthcoming

R Forrest, T Kennett and P Leather, *Home owners in negative equity*. School of Advanced Urban Studies, University of Bristol, 1994.

About one million households are experiencing negative equity, with mortgages that are greater than the value of their home. This study examines the characteristics of these households, drawing on data collected for a survey of housing in three localities – Glasgow, Luton and Bristol – supplemented with 30 depth interviews. It shows that people most likely to have negative equity were those who had bought their homes between 1988 and 1991, who were in social class A, and were couples without children. Negative equity had caused people to delay moving home, even turning down job opportunities. But they had not made significant attempts to increase their savings, nor had they modified their purchase of consumer durables.

Findings: HR 120 *Home owners in negative equity*

L Grant, *Disability and debt: the experience of disabled people in debt* Sheffield Citizen's Advice Bureaux Debt Support Unit, 1995.

Disabled people with problem debts regarded the experience of living with debt as the most significant aspect of their lives. Debt was usually the result of a combination of circumstances, often directly associated with disability but in the context of low income. Depth interviews were held in 76 households that had debts that they were unable to pay; 52 of the interviews were with disabled people and 24 with carers of one or more disabled people. They explored the causes and consequences of debt, as well as disabled people's experiences of dealing with their creditors and of seeking independent advice.

Findings: SP 78 *Debt and disability*

S Griffiths, *Supporting community care: the contribution of housing benefit*. National Institute for Social Work, 1995.

Housing Benefit plays an important role in supporting vulnerable people living in the community. But the link between Housing Benefit and community care is not recognised in either national policy or local practice. As a result, vulnerable people are left with inadequate financial resources to live on. That is the conclusion of this study which was based on depth interviews with Housing Benefit officers, advice workers, and care workers and postal surveys of carers. In addition to the research report, there is a separate report which sets out a policy agenda for central and local government to help them tackle the problem:

S Griffiths, *How Housing Benefit can work for community care.* Joseph Rownree Foundation, 1995.

Findings: HR 148 *The relationship between housing benefit and community care.*

A Herbert and E Kempson, *Water debt and disconnection.* Policy Studies Institute, 1995.

Almost two million households in Britain defaulted on their water bills in 1994, with low-income families with children running the greatest risk. This study examines who gets into debt and why; the water companies' approaches to debt recovery and disconnection; and customers' experiences of being disconnected from their water supply. It involved four linked surveys: a national survey of 2,000 households; a postal survey of all 31 water companies; depth telephone interviews with staff at 10 companies; and 39 depth interviews with households who had been disconnected.

Findings: SP 73 *Water debt and disconnection.*

A Herbert and E Kempson, *Credit use among ethnic minorities.* Policy Studies Institute, 1996.

Britain's ethnic minorities who live on low incomes are likely to have a high level of need for credit, which is unmet by high street credit institutions. This study describes the range of credit sources available to people living in three low-income minority ethnic communities (African Caribbean, Pakistani and Bangladeshi). It shows that all three communities had similar levels of need to borrow money and the money borrowed was used for broadly similar purposes. But they used different sources of borrowing to satisfy these needs. There was clear evidence that they were unable to gain access to high street credit and that this, in turn, led to people falling prey to lenders deploying questionable practices and to the communities themselves evolving informal savings and loans schemes. Islamic beliefs played a part, although this was not always as significant as was expected. Information was collected through depth interviews with community leaders and 51 people, of all ages and a range of family circumstances, who lived in the three communities.

Findings: Forthcoming

G Jones, *Family support for young people*, Family Policy Studies Centre, 1995.

Families are increasingly expected to provide financial support to young people and this can be crucial to those attempting to set up an independent home. This study was based on a national longitudinal survey of 4,000 young people in Scotland and follow-up interviews with 31 young people aged 21–22 years who had left home before the age of 19 and whose economic and family circumstances included a history of unemployment in the family or of family breakdown. It examines what happens when parents are unable or unwilling to help young people set up home on their own.

Findings: SP 70 Family support for young people setting up home

G Jones, *Leaving home*. Open University Press, 1995.

In recent years, young people have been leaving their parental home earlier. And the younger they leave home, the more they risk homelessness because their incomes are too low to give them access to the limited housing available. Many young people leave home because they are not getting on with their families, and are at greater risk of homelessness than those leaving for traditional reasons (to marry, to study or to take up a job). Returning home, too, has become more common, but many of those who were homeless said that they were unable to return home. This study included both 60 depth interviews and a longitudinal quantitative survey with homeless young people.

Findings: HR 108 Young people in and out of the housing market

P Kemp and P McLaverty, *Private tenants and restrictions in rent for housing benefit*. Centre for Housing Policy, University of York, 1995.

Local authorities restrict the amount of rent they take into account when calculating Housing Benefit if they consider the rent to be unreasonably high or the accommodation too large. This research involved an interview survey, in six local authority areas, with a total of 527 private tenants who were living in accommodation that had been referred to the rent officer in the previous 12 months. In addition, semi-structured interviews were carried out with 26 tenants whose rent had been restricted for Housing Benefit purposes.

Findings: HR 144 *Private tenants and restrictions in rent for housing benefit*

E Kempson, A Bryson and K Rowlingson, *Hard times? How poor families make ends meet.* Policy Studies Institute, 1994.

The need to make ends meet was a constant preoccupation for low-income families with children. Depth interviews with 74 families (40 of whom were lone parents) showed that a range of strategies were adopted by families in an attempt to balance the books – maximising income, adjusting patterns of money management and spending, turning to friends and relations and using consumer credit. Only a minority managed to avoid falling into arrears, but did so through self-denial, with a great cost in stress and ill-health

Findings: SP 53 Strategies used by low-income families with children to make ends meet

I Law, C Hylton, A Karmani and A Deacon, *Racial equality and social security service delivery: a study of the perceptions and experiences of black minority ethnic people eligible for benefit in Leeds.* University of Leeds, 1994 (Sociology and Social Policy Research Working Paper 10).

The Benefits Agency intention of improving the quality of benefit provision to minority ethnic claimants was impeded by the lack of knowledge about the differing perceptions of the claiming process held among these minority groups. Based on 155 semi-structured interviews and group discussions, this research studied the perceptions and experiences of both claimants and non-claimants from five minority groups (Indians, Chinese, Pakistani and Bangladeshi Muslims, and African Caribbeans).

Findings: SP 59 The provision of social security benefits to minority ethnic communities

S Middleton, K Ashworth and R Walker, *Family fortunes: pressures on parents and children in the 1990s*. Child Poverty Action Group, 1994.

There are many economic and social pressures, on both parents and children, for children to be able to participate fully in the community in which they live and to have access to the same opportunities as other children with whom they play or go to school. This study has explored how parents and children cope with these pressures. It was based on 22 group discussions with 193 mothers, selected from across the socio-economic spectrum, and interviews and group discussions with a total of 240 (unrelated) children. The mothers also discussed minimum standards for a child's 'physical, mental, spiritual, moral and social development' – a right asserted by the United Nations Convention on the Rights of the Child. The costs of these exceeded current benefit levels by between 11 and 56 per cent.

Findings: SP 67 Attitudes to spending on children

L Morris and J Ritchie, *Income maintenance and living standards*. Social and Community Planning Research, 1994.

High levels of unemployment mean that large numbers of households live on social security benefits for long periods of time, yet there is a lack of up-to-date research looking at living standards of these benefit recipients. Sixty depth interviews compared the living standards of families with dependent children who were: unemployed and claiming Income Support; claiming in-work benefits; receiving the male median wage. This showed that, although there was a gradual upward shift in standards of living across the three groups, only the median earners group achieved a reasonable level of comfort. Those on benefits faced competing demands from buying food, children's clothing and paying regular bills. Debt and using credit were commonplace.

Findings: SP 65 Income maintenance and living standards.

N Pleace, *Housing vulnerable single homeless people*. Centre for Housing Policy, University of York, 1995.

Many statutorily homeless people have a range of housing and support needs, yet these needs were often not met. The study examined the rehousing of statutorily homeless single people by four urban local authority housing departments, interviewing housing staff and 62 single homeless people in depth. It found that there was an inadequate supply of suitable temporary or permanent housing. Moreover, in addition to shelter, homeless people needed help and support with health care; their finances, including welfare rights advice; daily life skills; and social and emotional relationships. If these non-housing needs are not met, rehousing can be unsuccessful. The profound needs of this group caused housing management problems for local authorities. Housing department staff reported feeling under pressure to provide these support services themselves and frequently did so. But this could only be on a limited basis.

Findings: HR 153 *Housing vulnerable single homeless people.*

A Power and R Tunstall, *Swimming against the tide: polarisation or progress on 20 unpopular council estates, 1980–1995.* Joseph Rowntree Foundation, 1995.

Over the 1980s, social polarisation – particularly on large unpopular council estates – became extreme. This long-term study shows how 20 of the most unpopular council estates in the country were restored from extreme social, physical and management problems. It draws on data collected in earlier studies in 1981 and 1987 and updates it with observations and interviews with 131 tenants and 62 staff. These showed that improvements were achieved through continuous, locally based, intensive, hands-on management and tenant involvement.

Findings: HR 151 *Progress and polarisation on 20 council estates.*

C Roaf and C Lloyd, *Multi-agency work with young people in difficulty?* Oxford Brookes University, 1995.

Young people have multiple needs and require the services of more than one agency, yet this study found no one agency with responsibility for co-ordinating services for this group. Young people were helped according to how they fitted into the work of agencies, rather than by an analysis of what help they needed. As a consequence they tended to be seen as on the margin, or outside of, any one particular service. This study involved interviews in 70 agencies working with young people in Oxford and depth interviews with 15 young people. Thirty young homeless people contributed to the research by sharing their past experiences with different agencies.

Findings: SCR 68 *Multi-agency work with young people in difficulty*

K Rowlingson, *Moneylenders and their customers*. Policy Studies Institute, 1994.

An estimated 1,200 licensed moneylending companies employ 27,000 collectors who visit three million customers in their homes each week. Research involving non-participant observation and depth interviews with eight collectors and 31 customers provided a detailed insight into this aspect of the credit market. It showed that customers often had limited access to other sources of credit; that costs of loans from moneylenders were high; but that the image of moneylenders portrayed by the media was often far from reality. The majority of collectors are women and their business tends to be built on friendship rather than fear. At the same time the study showed that there are groups that even licensed moneylenders are reluctant to accept as new customers: long-term unemployed, lone parents, pensioners and those living in areas with high levels of crime.

J Rugg and L Sanderling, *Evaluation of access schemes*. Centre for Housing Policy, University of York (Forthcoming).

People living on a low income can face a number of barriers to renting in the private sector: the limited availabilty of affordable, single person accommodation; landlords' unwillingness to let to people on Housing Benefit; and difficulty with paying rent in advance and bonds. A number of schemes to help people surmount these difficulties have been established by local authorities and voluntary sector agencies. This study has evaluated 148 of these schemes which offered two types of service: accommodation registers, matching appropriate vacancies with prospective tenants, and advance payments schemes, which help with rent in advance or bonds by offering cash or loans, or arranging written guarantees for the landlord.

Findings: Forthcoming

M Shucksmith, P Chapman and G Clark, *Disadvantage in rural Scotland: how is it experienced and how can it be tackled?* Summary report. Rural Forum, 1994.

Many people living in rural Scotland were experiencing poverty and deprivation, but rejected the objective assessment of their situation. Rather, the vast majority felt that they were advantaged by their rural lifestyle. A questionnaire survey with 500 households, followed by 120 depth interviews, showed that poverty and disadvantage were widespread in rural Scotland but conventional indicators failed to capture most dimensions of rural disadvantage. Take-up of benefits was low; lack of affordable housing was a pervasive problem; employment opportunities were very limited; and general service provision was a matter of concern.

Findings: SP 62 *Disadvantage in rural Scotland*

S Speak, S Cameron, R Woods and R Gilroy, *Young single mothers: barriers to independent living*. Family Policy Studies Centre, 1995.

Young single mothers often found themselves catapulted simultaneously into independent adulthood and motherhood. Furthermore, many had to come to terms with their new role and endeavour to establish an independent home quickly and with limited family support. This study explored, through 40 depth interviews and 15 group discussions, the main problems for young mothers trying to establish a secure and suitable home for themselves and their children. Most faced difficulty finding suitable housing near their families and needed to use credit to furnish their homes.

Findings: SP 72 *The difficulties of setting up home for young single mothers.*

H Third, *Affordable childcare and housing: a case study of tenants of a black housing association.* Centre for Housing Policy, University of York, 1995.

Housing association rents have risen rapidly since the late 1980s, resulting in fears that they are now beyond the means of those on low wages, without benefit support. Childcare, even following the government's 'childcare disregard' initiative, remains a major expense for prospective workers. Depth interviews with 41 mothers (one-third Asian, one-third African Caribbean and one-third white) examined how mothers perceive and respond to these two work disincentives.

Findings: SP 79 *Affordable childcare and housing*